GO FURTHER WITH GOD

GO
FURTHER
GOD
WITH

S. RENEE SMITH &
WILLIAM J. SMITH, SR.

To my wife, Shirley M. Smith, my partner in poverty, prayer, and progress. You stood beside me when all I had was a dream. You never pulled back; you pressed forward with faith—carrying more than your share so I could carry mine. Every page is evidence that God is with us.

All my love, William

To my husband, HL, you're a force of nature—a presence that steadies me, strengthens me, and makes space for all of who I am and what I'm called to do.

To my mom, Shirley M. Smith, your faith in God is firm. Your love, prayers, and support carry us all.

To my readers and friends, I pray that the words on these pages offer you divine clarity, holy courage, and a nudge toward your next step.

With love, S. Renee

CONTENTS

My father shared the stories.
I interpreted and wrote them.

Together, we invite you on a sacred journey—
one of faith shaped by trials,
purpose revealed through pain,
and grace that never ends.

This book didn't begin as a collection of memories.
It began as a testimony—
of how God shapes a life,
not all at once,
but moment by moment,
in the quiet, the breaking, and the becoming.

WHY THIS BOOK

S. RENEE SMITH, AUTHOR

AN UNEXPECTED JOURNEY

Writing this book changed me

Have you ever taken a path, believing it would be one thing, only to discover something entirely different? Yet, once you took that first step, you knew you were doing the right thing at the right time.

As a coach, I knew writing my dad's story would change him, but I didn't foresee the profound impact it would have on me.

The journey of writing *Go Further with God* has been unlike anything I imagined. I've stepped into the stories of a man, my father, whom I've known my entire life, yet I now see him through an entirely new lens.

I've captured his strength, along with his vulnerabilities, his walk with God, and the raw, human moments that have shaped him.

I had heard my dad share some of these stories before, but never quite like this. Now, I truly understand the weight they carry, the prayers behind the decisions, and the silent battles he never spoke of until now.

This process has matured me spiritually. I carry a peace I have never known. I see myself, and others, through a gentler, wiser lens. My view of business, purpose, and legacy has shifted, now shaped by grace and conviction. I'm more aware of how God moves, more grounded in how I respond to people and pain, and more anchored in His greater plan. My understanding of what it means to *go further with God* is now richer and deeply personal.

I didn't just write a book with my father; I have been transformed by it.

I believe that as you engage with each lesson and reflect on your own journey, you will experience something similar—a shift in how you see yourself, your story, and your relationship with God.

A FATHER'S EARLY LESSON
Childhood memory, timeless wisdom

My father has been one of my greatest teachers.

Growing up with three brothers meant constant teasing. When their playful jabs became too much, I'd run to my dad for help.

"Daddy, he's making faces at me!" I'd whine, hoping he would step in.

He'd calmly reply, "How do you know he's making faces at you? You must be looking at him."

Translation: Stop looking at him, and you won't see his face.

At the time, I sought protection. But my father offered me something greater: a lifelong lesson in self-awareness and personal power. He didn't rescue me from discomfort; he taught me how to rise above it.

SPACE HELD US
From cradle to confidence

As an infant, I refused to sleep unless I was nestled between my parents. I'm not sure whether my father saw it as an intrusion or a safety concern, but the moment I fell asleep, he would place me back in the bassinet. I would immediately wake up and cry until he returned me to his arms.

By my first birthday, I began to withdraw from him completely, perhaps unconsciously viewing his boundaries as a form of rejection.

Then, around age three, everything shifted.

One evening, he sat on the fireplace hearth. Without hesitation, I climbed into his lap. He smiled and gestured to my mother without saying a word. Today, he says of that moment, "You've never left."

Over time, we discovered a deeper truth about who we could be for one another and to one another. Our relationship has evolved, growing into one marked by mutual respect, laughter, and honest conversations. We have shared joy, disappointment, and the kind of truth that does not divide but deepens love.

IMPERFECT PEOPLE

Faithful heart, imperfect hands

My father isn't perfect; he's flawed, just like you and me. But as his daughter, I've learned a spiritual truth: God doesn't require perfection to do perfect work through us. He desires a willing heart, the humility to listen, and the courage to act.

Watching my father handle difficult people and navigate challenging situations has taught me the value of understanding a person's heart rather than judging their behavior. He stays aligned with God through deep empathy and compassion. Many have said they could never demonstrate the same level of restraint he shows.

I describe him as disciplined and grounded, carrying himself with confidence rooted in conviction. When he makes a mistake, he owns it. But he refuses to be held captive by his past, just as he won't hold others to theirs.

As shared in Chapter 5, he once hired a man who had fired him and another who had refused to help him—not out of revenge, but from a place of grace. He didn't hold a grudge; he made room for God to do something redemptive.

When I felt unsure or questioned my next step, his confidence in me gave me the courage to continue. And when I felt like stepping back instead of stepping up because of what people were saying, he would remind me: "Let people run their mouths. You run your business."

BEYOND THE PEDESTAL
Shattered illusions, deeper love

I remember giving a presentation early in my speaking career. Afterward, my father came over. I could feel his excitement and pride. He hugged me and said, "I've heard some of the best speakers in the world, and you're among them."

I didn't fully believe him, not because I thought he was being insincere, but because I hadn't yet embraced my talent or trusted myself enough to accept his confidence in what he saw in me.

Still, his words lingered.

His faith in me reminded me that belief doesn't always come with applause. Sometimes, it comes in the steady presence of someone who sees what you can't see in yourself.

For all the good qualities my father possesses, I've realized how easy it is to place people we love and admire on a pedestal—a place meant only for God. When we finally recognize their humanity, it's not the person who crumbles; it's the illusion we built around who we believed they were. What truly breaks is the expectation that a title or role should make someone perfect—perfect by our standards, shaped by our needs.

It's easy to misinterpret actions, take words out of context, and forget that growth—both theirs and ours—often comes from learning from mistakes. We must celebrate the divine moments in each other while honoring the humanity we all share. That's how we give grace, and that's how we receive it.

I'm still learning that it's possible to hold admiration and realism at the same time, and that grace is what bridges the gap between the two.

LEARN THROUGH LIFE
Legacy, aging, and sacred moments

It seems I've always appreciated the fragility of life and the passage of time. That's why I began recording my father's stories over a decade ago. But as I watched my parents grow older, I found myself taking a deeper breath, noticing their steps slow, their hearing fade, and their minds lose sharpness. These observations have made each moment feel heavier—not only with meaning, but with the quiet ache of knowing that nothing lasts forever.

Over twenty years ago, I told my father that I was afraid of losing him. His response was calm and reassuring:

> "We all must go and make room for new people to come in; otherwise, the world would become overpopulated."

In that moment, I realized my fear wasn't just about losing him; it was about losing what was familiar and anchoring.

It's a brutal truth to accept, but I now understand what my father has been trying to teach me before he leaves this world, if I don't go before him, and what God continues to reveal: loss isn't the end. It's the beginning of something new, something grander. If we allow it, loss becomes a sacred invitation to discover a higher level of ourselves.

GOD'S ALREADY IN WHAT COMES NEXT
This is bigger than one story

No matter how much we resist accepting loss—whether it's the death of a loved one, the end of a relationship, or the conclusion of a career chapter—faith reminds us that God is already present in what comes next. This captures the essence of *Go Further with God*.

It's not just about sharing my father's story; it's about recognizing ourselves in his journey. It shows how God shapes us through our challenges, anchors us in His presence, and guides us toward purpose—even when life doesn't go as planned.

You will read raw, real stories filled with grace—stories that defy logic yet ignite faith. They will prompt you to look deeper, reflect more sincerely, and believe more boldly.

I'm honored to walk this journey with you, and I pray that as you read, you begin to see how far you can go when you choose to accept God's invitation to go further with Him.

With every turn of the page, may you feel His presence, hear His whisper, and follow the path He has already prepared for you.

I'll be walking with you, heart open and faith forward, as together we go further with God.

S. Renee Smith

WHY I SHARED MY STORY, AND WHAT I HOPE YOU'LL SEE IN YOURS

WILLIAM J. SMITH, SR., STORYTELLER

DEFINING MOMENTS, LASTING IMPACT

One decision changed everything

Have you ever looked back on your life and wondered where you'd be if you had taken a different path? It's remarkable how a single decision can shape the course of our lives: our work, our relationships, even the person we marry.

The choices we make often reflect what's happening inside us—our desires, fears, and anxieties. Beneath the surface, beliefs quietly guide our lives in ways we don't always recognize. But when we pause to reflect, our choices can reveal deeper truths about who we are becoming—and perhaps who God is calling us to be.

One pivotal moment came when I had to choose between staying in a situation that compromised my values or taking a leap of faith to start my own business. That decision changed everything I believed—and became the unexpected catalyst for a faith I didn't know I needed.

Every day, we make choices—some trivial, others life-changing. Since retiring in 2011, I have taken time to reflect on the decisions that have shaped my journey. Each one has become part of the tapestry of my life, woven with lessons, faith, and growth.

I have come this far because there is a God. I chose to accept Jesus Christ as my Lord and Savior. Guided by God's wisdom, I became a contractor capable of designing and building homes and commercial properties, even though I did not finish high school. Instead, I relied on His guidance.

One morning at 3 a.m., feeling discouraged because I could not understand a blueprint (Chapter 4, Lesson 10), I had a dream. In it, God showed me how to read a blueprint and figure a construction bid. I woke up with a clear understanding, knowing exactly what steps to take. That miraculous moment confirmed for me that God is real. You will see Him when you trust that He is there.

LESSONS THROUGH LIFE AND LOSS
God's vision outlasts our plans

Not every lesson was easy. I lost my business when a client declared bankruptcy. I had to adapt when agreements fell through. I even left a job because of discrimination. But through it all, I realized something important: our plans are often just our desires written down in detail.

God's vision always goes beyond ours. Within it lies the truth of our purpose and the power to accomplish what we never thought possible.

We often think we need to control every detail. But faith is not about control; it is about surrender, vision, and the willingness to listen and act. God does not need our plans, nor does He ask for them. He simply asks for our trust. And when we walk with Him, He brings the right people, the right opportunities, and the right timing.

I remember when a construction manager turned me down, convinced I couldn't finance my $1 million portion of a multi-million-dollar project

(Chapter 6, Lesson 16). I asked, "If my suppliers commit to providing everything I need, would that change your decision?" He called a supplier, who confirmed I had access to $10 million in materials if needed.

That is favor—God working through people to fulfill His plan. Not because I earned it, but because He ordained it. Favor isn't about being liked; it's about being positioned and propelled forward by divine grace through the hands and hearts of others. And we know, of course, that it is God who is using them.

FAITH IS A JOURNEY, NOT A SHORTCUT
Grace shows up, even in our messes

I have not lived a perfect life. I have made poor choices, spoken words I regret, and started fires only God's grace could extinguish. Yet even in the messes I created, His grace guided me to higher ground and kept me moving forward. That is not a cliché; it is the truth.

I am not here to give you a blueprint for life. What I can offer are spiritual insights and lessons I have learned through experience—truths that have strengthened my walk with God and shaped my path.

The most important truth I have learned is this: God meets you where you are. If you give Him your heart and take that first step in faith, He will handle the rest.

YOU ARE NOT ALONE
God is with you always

God prepares us to carry what we pray for. He speaks through everything, but if you do not pay attention, you notice nothing. Some lessons took years to understand, and I am still learning. For decades, I did not think anyone needed to hear my story, but now I see how every trial, blessing, and silent moment has something to teach.

I want you to remember:

1. **You're not alone.** You may feel isolated at times, but God is with you—even when you feel overlooked or ignored. He was there, He is here, He lives within you.

2. **Don't quit.** Life gets tough. But giving up won't make things easier. Nothing is so heavy that you should walk away from the journey. Pause. Rest. Pray. Then keep moving forward.

3. **Own your choices.** Your decisions matter. You are accountable for them all—even the ones that didn't turn out as you hoped. When you take responsibility, you create space for growth and healing.

4. **Have faith.** God is at work, even when it seems like things are falling apart. His plan is greater than yours.

WHAT I HOPE YOU TAKE AWAY
Lessons worth carrying

This is not just a book of stories; it is a series of lessons drawn from a life that began with uncertainty, missteps, and a search for something more. What I lived through isn't so different from what many experience, but I now see how my decisions shaped the road ahead in ways I could never have imagined possible. Some of those choices made life harder, yet even then, God was already at work.

My daughter, S. Renee, helped me put these lessons into words, but the truth in them belongs to anyone willing to trust God. I have lived long enough to know that challenges will come, but God never fails. If you are willing to listen—not just to these words, but to what God is saying through them—there is something here for you.

Whatever you are facing, or no matter what you have endured, remember this: God is with you, for you, and within you. Do not get stuck in what you could have or should have done. Trust in God's will, rest in His timing, and believe that everything will fall into place, including you.

If you do, you will *Go Further with God*.

Still learning. Still trusting. Always believing.

William J. Smith, Sr.

HOW TO
USE THIS BOOK

You've just received an invitation. Now, here's how to walk through this journey intentionally.

WHAT YOU'LL FIND IN EACH CHAPTER

Each chapter begins with **S. Renee's Moments to Measure**—a spiritually centered reflection that introduces the key theme in the upcoming lessons, providing emotional context and spiritual clarity. A related scripture grounds the lesson in God's Word.

Each chapter features three lessons that include:

- **A grounding scripture** anchors the message in biblical truth.

- **A true story** is drawn from real-life experience—honest, raw, and spiritually significant.

- **Pause + Reflect** offers a brief devotional insight to help you see how God might be at work in your life.

- **Reflection Prompts** present three questions designed to guide you toward spiritual clarity, emotional growth, and closer alignment with God's will, while also helping you identify your next steps.

In the final lesson, instead of **Pause + Reflect** and **Reflection Prompts**, we conclude with a blessing and an invitation—giving you space to consider your next step with God.

PRACTICES TO STRENGTHEN YOUR RELATIONSHIP

These lessons are offered to you as pathways—not prescriptions—for drawing nearer to God through personal reflection, honest conversation, and active listening. Use them in the way that feels most meaningful for your journey.

Journaling

Writing can reveal what God has been showing you all along. As you read and respond to the **Reflection Prompts**, consider journaling your thoughts, emotions, and prayers. Over time, you might start noticing patterns of growth, healing, or moments that you once missed—moments where God could have been gently trying to get your attention.

Group/Partner Use

Whether in a small group, virtual circle, or with a trusted friend, consider discussing one or two lessons each week. Sharing your reflections with others can deepen insight, spark courage, and foster spiritual accountability.

Author's Note: The events in this book are based on the true experiences of William J. Smith, Sr., and the reflections of his daughter, S. Renee Smith. While every effort has been made to recount them accurately, some names have been changed to protect privacy, and certain dates are approximate due to the passage of time. What remains constant is the heart of each story and the enduring truth of how God moved through it.

Unless otherwise noted, all Scripture quotations are from the New Living Translation (NLT).

CHAPTER 1

GOD'S PRESENCE IN OUR PAIN

GOD'S HAND IN DEFINING MOMENTS

Don't be afraid, for I am with you.
Don't be discouraged, for I am your God.
I will strengthen you and help you.
I will hold you up with my victorious right hand.

ISAIAH 41:10

S. RENEE'S MOMENTS TO MEASURE

CHAPTER 1

Every story you carry holds more than memory; it holds meaning. Your experiences, endurance, and questions shape who you are becoming. When you pause to examine your story, you may begin to see how even the painful moments were preparing you for a greater purpose.

God's Presence in Our Pain invites you to consider that God doesn't only appear after the pain is over; He is present within it. He meets us in the dark corners of fear, in the weight of our wondering, and in the moments when we feel most alone, with healing, provision, and redirection.

In Lessons 1–3, you'll learn:

- Fear may speak loudly, but it does not speak for God.

- God often provides what you need before you even realize you need it.

- Healing and redirection are among God's clearest demonstrations of His presence.

- You don't have to understand how God is working to be entirely covered by His love.

GOD HEALS

FAITH ASKED, GRACE ANSWERED

I will give you back your health and heal
your wounds, says the Lord.

JEREMIAH 30:17

GOD'S MERCY

I used to believe I wouldn't live past my fifties—not because I wanted to die, but because I had accepted a lie. Yet here I am, in my mid-eighties, realizing how unfounded that fear was. I had no evidence; it was just a thought I chose to believe.

Still, I've had close calls—jumping from a collapsing scaffold, making critical mistakes while operating 18,000-pound machinery, and facing other dangerous situations caused by human error.

I remember working on a three-story commercial building. My skilled crew had set up the scaffold, and everything appeared in order. We'd done this kind of job many times before. I trusted them, but that misplaced confidence nearly cost us our lives.

The scaffold had been built using hollow 4-inch blocks instead of the solid ones that should have been used. I climbed up and began working. Suddenly, I felt something shift beneath my feet. It was gradual—too subtle to raise alarm at first—until I looked down and saw the scaffold beginning to give way. Quiet. Unmistakable.

My heart began to race.

I didn't think; I shouted, "Get out of the way!"

As the scaffold continued to buckle, I stepped onto the block wall we had built, and the scaffold collapsed.

No one was hurt. I knew it was God. Psalm 91:11 says, "For he will order his angels to protect you wherever you go."

My crew and I didn't just survive that fall: God commanded His angels to catch what I couldn't for more than thirty years of running a construction business. He is merciful and loves us. That's why I'm still here.

A MOTHER'S FAITH

God's protection over my life didn't begin in adulthood; it started long before I ever stepped onto a jobsite. The fact that I can walk remains one of the most significant miracles in my life, a constant reminder of the power of faith and grace.

According to my mother, everything seemed normal from the day I was born until I was about eighteen months old. I reached all the usual developmental milestones, including learning to walk. But one day, when she came to lift me from my crib, she found me lying on my back with my legs curled tightly toward my torso.

Concerned, she tried to straighten them, but they would snap back to the curled position. After several days of worry, she took me to the doctor, who suspected polio. At the time, polio was known to affect children under five, often causing pain in the limbs and, in rare cases, permanent paralysis, especially in the legs.

I was tested, and thankfully, the results came back negative. The doctor had no explanation and told my mother I would never walk again.

Every day, she prayed, gently applied ointment to my legs, and stretched them straight. But they would always spring back into place. Still, she never gave up. She kept up the routine, determined to ease whatever pain I might have been feeling but couldn't express.

Then, just after my second birthday, something incredible happened. One day, as she passed the crib, she saw me standing—ready to climb out and go play outside.

Hopeful but cautious, she gently lifted me and slowly lowered me to the floor, letting my feet touch down. To her amazement, they did. Feeling both disbelief and joy, she gradually removed her hands from beneath my arms, and I began walking toward the door.

At our next visit, the doctor still had no explanation. But my mother was convinced that God had performed a miracle. When she shared the story with me, I knew it was my first miracle, although it wouldn't be my last.

And I'm grateful for that—because just a few years later, I would need another one.

BAREFOOT AND BLEEDING

When I was about seven years old, I faced a different kind of threat—one that could have cost me my leg and possibly my life.

We were living in Mims, Florida. My father had a contract to clear the orange groves after the fruit was harvested, and he brought my mother, my brother, and me along to help. Despite my age and the risks, I worked barefoot, using a sharp hoe to cut through the thick grass root beneath the trees. At some point, I cut myself. I didn't even notice. I didn't feel it.

I was still playing and laughing with my brother when my mother suddenly asked, "Where is that blood coming from?"

We stopped, and started watching her scan the ground. She followed the trail of blood through the grass to where I stood. I looked up at her as she looked at me. Then I glanced down and slowly lifted my pant leg.

I had cut through the bone in my right ankle.

From just above my calf down to my ankle, my leg had turned white. I looked up again and saw my mother's face; she looked like she had seen a ghost.

She ran over to me.

"What happened?" she asked urgently.

I started to feel upset, not because it hurt, but because she seemed frightened. "I don't know," I said.

As she kept staring at my leg, I added, "I don't remember."

When she asked again, I nodded and told her, "It doesn't hurt. I can't feel anything."

She panicked. "Don't move," she said. "I'm going to get your daddy. I'll be right back."

She took off running; within minutes, she was back with my dad, who looked at the wound and said nothing.

She said, "He needs to go to the hospital."

My father nodded. "I'll take him."

"I'm going with you," she said.

"No," he replied. "You stay here and watch the workers. I'll take him."

Disappointment crossed her face, but she agreed. Hopping on my left leg, I followed my dad to the truck.

As we drove down the road, he asked, "Bill, does it hurt?"

I replied, "No, it doesn't hurt."

He stopped at a drugstore, bought some supplies, treated my wound, wrapped it up, and we went back to work. When we returned, I remember my mother being upset that he hadn't taken me to the hospital for proper treatment. They exchanged words. I don't believe my father meant to do me harm; he just didn't trust doctors.

So my mother took over. She cared for my wound, applying ointment, gauze, and prayer.

Not a day passed without her tending to it. But that didn't stop the long and painful road to healing.

Looking back, I realize the pain wasn't just physical. It carried a weight I couldn't name at the time. It reminds me of how Job described his suffering in Job 30:30: "My skin has turned dark, and my bones burn with fever." Imagine being in so much pain that it becomes unbearable to live in your own body. That's exactly how I felt.

At first, it looked like the wound was healing. The skin began to close, but underneath, the tissue was rotting. The pain was excruciating, and the smell was overwhelming. I could be in one room, and you'd smell it from another.

My mother cleaned and wrapped it every day, sometimes more than once. But each time someone stepped on it, the skin peeled off again. What we didn't understand was that the damage ran deeper. The real danger was happening beneath the surface.

Based on what I've read since, I now believe the tissue in my ankle had started to die—a process called necrosis. When blood flow is cut off, the tissue doesn't get the oxygen it needs and begins to decay from the inside out. That's why it started to rot.

The smell didn't come from the wound alone; it came from bacteria feeding on dead tissue. Once that process begins, the body struggles to heal because the infection and dead cells prevent the wound from closing properly. That's why every time someone accidentally stepped on it, the skin tore away again. It wasn't healing—it was decaying.

Days turned into weeks, weeks into months, but my mother never stopped. Her hands, her heart, and her prayers carried me through. Nearly a year later, the wound finally healed, although the swelling never completely went away and the scar is still visible.

God saved my leg—and my life. I kept walking. Maybe it's the unexamined life that convinces us to believe the lie.

Could two health crises within seven years have led me to believe I wouldn't live past fifty? Was the unresolved trauma from my childhood woven into my beliefs, reinforcing the idea that I was destined to leave behind a young family to navigate life without me?

Reflecting on my mother's faith and prayerful life until her passing at age ninety-one, I wonder if her persistent prayers during my early years planted a deep connection to God in my spirit. I've always sensed a presence, a feeling of protection, and a calling—even when I didn't fully understand God or what it meant to be surrounded by His kindness.

Still, growing up and watching my mother, I learned this: if I believe there is a God, I should trust that He hears my prayers, and I should not impose my own limitations or expectations on what His answer should be or how it should look.

PAUSE + REFLECT

God's healing power doesn't always look the same. Sometimes, it comes suddenly and unmistakably—a miracle that defies logic. Other times, it unfolds slowly, hidden beneath layers of pain, or begins long before you even realize you need it.

It may show up in the body as a protective response to danger, or through the love of someone who refuses to give up: a mother who prays day after day over her child battling addiction, trusting God for what medicine and intervention alone cannot provide.

Maybe you've heard the words, "There's nothing more we can do." Maybe you've endured pain that refuses to leave or carry beliefs still waiting to be healed. Remember this: God still heals—in His timing, in His way, often quietly, long before you're aware.

His grace steps in when your confidence runs out.

REFLECTION PROMPTS

- Have you ever gone through a healing that didn't occur all at once but gradually, and sometimes painfully? What lessons did you take from it?

_____

_____

_____

- What false beliefs about your body, worth, or future have you held, and how have they influenced your journey?

  _____

  _____

  _____

- Who has prayed for you, cared for you, or stood by you when you couldn't help yourself? How has their faith influenced yours?

  _____

  _____

  _____

GOD PROVIDES

PROVISION WITHOUT A PLAN

For I know the plans I have for you, says the Lord.
They are plans for good and not for disaster,
to give you a future and a hope.

JEREMIAH 29:11

LEAVING WITH NOTHING

By fifteen, I was overwhelmed with emotions, caught between my father's expectations and my own desires and beliefs. He expected me to work hard and hand over all my earnings to support the family. While I didn't mind helping, being forced to work without keeping anything for myself made me feel like nothing more than free labor. Still, I didn't say a word, it was his house, and those were his rules.

Throughout my life, I never confronted, argued with, or talked back to my parents. But being unable to express myself left me feeling trapped in a world that wasn't my own. I was suffocating my true self, quietly yearning for freedom. Have you ever felt that way?

For nearly a year, I thought about leaving home. I didn't know where I would go or how I would survive—I just knew I had a strong need to escape. After many long silent conversations with myself, I finally made the decision to leave, vowing never to return to live under my parents' roof again.

Deciding to go was easy. Figuring out when was harder. I was a minor, just starting ninth grade. If I stayed in Delaware, my father could easily find me and force me to return home. I couldn't risk being seen. So I told no one—not my siblings, not a soul. I ran away less than thirty days after my sixteenth birthday in November 1955. No plan. No food. No bag.

I waited until 2 a.m., knowing my father always stayed up late. When I was sure he was asleep, I quietly lifted the window, careful not to wake my brothers, and climbed out. Beneath the dark, faintly starlit sky and cool autumn air, with just the clothes on my back, I felt nothing. I was more in my head than in my heart. As I walked north beneath the vastness of God's creation, I felt a sense of peace.

As the hours passed, my stomach ached and my throat went dry. I suddenly remembered something my father used to say: "Beg, borrow, but never steal." That was when it hit me: I needed to figure out how I was going to eat.

THE FIRST RIDE NORTH

Without a watch, I could only guess the time by the sun's position. As dawn broke and traffic picked up, I raised my thumb, hoping someone would stop to give me a ride.

Before long, a middle-aged White man pulled over and asked, "Where are you headed?"

I replied, "As far as you'll take me."

"You can ride as far as I'm going," he replied, "but tell me where you want to get dropped off before I exit."

It was safer back then, so I gladly hopped in after walking for hours.

He wasn't much of a talker, and neither was I. After a while, he asked, "Where are you headed?"

"I don't know," I said. "North. Hoping to find work."

As we drove, I realized we were on the New Jersey Turnpike, somewhere between Delaware and New York, though I had no idea exactly where.

When we neared his exit, he slowed the car. "This is where I gotta let you out," he said.

He pulled over. I thanked him, and he nodded. "Take care of yourself."

We parted ways and continued on our own paths.

I kept walking north until another vehicle pulled over. An older White gentleman asked if I needed a ride, and I accepted his offer to go farther north. We drove for a short distance before I noticed signs for the New York state line.

My hunger and the silence in the first car had given me time to think about how I would survive with the limited knowledge I had. As a migrant farm worker moving from state to state with my father and family, I had spent most of my life working on potato farms—that was all I knew.

Watching my father work as a crew leader taught me that success depends on what you can contribute. Thinking about that made me realize I could get a job picking potatoes.

This driver was a bit more talkative than the first. He asked, "Where are you going?"

I proudly said, "I'm going where they pick potatoes."

"Oh, they pick potatoes in Long Island," he replied.

Perfect, I thought. I finally had a place where I could put my skills to work. As we approached the area, it looked familiar—a potato belt.

Without me asking, he kindly drove me straight to a potato farm and dropped me off at the end of the road around 1 p.m. I had traveled safely for eleven hours since climbing out of my bedroom window in Delaware to where I would begin my new life in Long Island, New York.

POTATOES AND PROVISION

I walked up the driveway, with the garage ahead and the house to the right. I felt confident, hopeful, and relieved to be in a place that felt familiar.

A warm voice called out, "How can I help you?"

"I'm a little hungry," I blurted, "but I'm willing to work for a meal."

Without hesitation, the farmer went into the house and quickly returned with a plate of food. He invited me to sit on a bench near the garage, and I savored each bite as the weight of my journey began to lift.

He might have been watching me through the window because he came back just as I finished.

Personable and friendly, he sat on the bench across from me and asked, "What's your name?"

"William," I said.

"William, I'm Mr. Miller."

Curiously, he asked, "William, what can you do?"

Excited by his question, I proudly replied, "I can pick potatoes."

"You've come to the right place," he said with a smile.

He explained that I would earn eight cents for every bag of potatoes I picked, lifted, and loaded onto the truck, but I would lose two cents for each bag I couldn't lift and load. After our talk, I headed to the field, scanning the long rows of potatoes and noticing the other workers.

Some were older and fragile, others younger and less physically capable. I figured someone would have to help them get their bags onto the truck. I immediately started thinking about how I could earn more by not only doing my work but also helping others with theirs.

At the end of my first day, Mr. Miller and his wife pulled me aside. They explained that they didn't want me to sleep in the labor camp with the other workers. Labor camps are typically cramped housing shared by migrant workers, with limited facilities and little privacy.

Instead, they offered to convert their garage into a room just for me. Looking back, I wonder if they suspected I was underage and wanted to protect me. Whatever their reason, I believe it was God's favor.

Without delay, Mr. Miller backed the car out of the garage and waved for me to follow him to the barn.

Pointing at a couch, he said, "Grab the other end."

Together, we carried it into the garage. He showed me how to use the existing heater and mentioned he would be adding a wood stove in a few days. To me, it felt like a five-star hotel.

It was a welcome change from traveling with my family between states for work, cleaning chicken coops and setting up partitions to separate the males from the females. Then, we used scraps of clothing to cushion ourselves from the hard ground as we slept.

Lying on that couch, wrapped in warmth and comfort, I asked myself, *Why me?* It's a question I've continued to ask over the years. The feeling is still strange—and humbling. But that favor seems to have followed me all my life. Maybe you've felt it too—that kind of favor that didn't make sense, but somehow found you right where you were.

RETURNING HOME

During my time in Long Island, I stayed focused, completed my work, and often helped others with theirs. Ironically, I earned more money assisting them than I did from my own workload. When potato season ended in late September or early October, I caught a ride south with a coworker.

As we approached Delaware, I asked him to drop me off at a Chevrolet dealership about fifteen miles north of my parents' house. Even though I had left home with nothing, I knew I had to return with something to show for the year I was away—proof of growth and productivity.

I searched the lot for an affordable car and found a 1952 green Chevy with a six-cylinder engine. I paid cash and proudly drove to my parents' house. When I pulled into the driveway, they rushed outside to greet me. We went inside, and though the moment felt a little strange at first, we quickly settled into warm conversation, talking for hours as if I had never left.

The only sign I had been gone for a year was when I stood to leave.

My father immediately stood and said, "It's good to have you home, Son."

"I'm not coming back home, Diddy," I replied. "I'm only here to visit."

My mother asked softly and angelically, "You won't be staying with us?"

Mirroring her gentleness, I replied, "No, Muh, I'm not."

As I spoke those words, I still felt nothing—no anger, no guilt—only a firm belief that peace meant maintaining distance. Although I knew staying absent from their lives wasn't the right decision, I was asserting my independence and reaffirming a vow I had made to myself a year earlier: I would never live in my parents' house again.

It would take time—and a lot of living—to understand what was happening within me back then. I can now see that God was always with me, even when I felt alone. His guidance showed up in ways I didn't always recognize, especially during the most difficult moments.

My mother used to say, "God has His hands on you." I didn't understand what that meant at the time, unable to grasp her faith or see what she saw in me. Now, I can only imagine what she carried—what she whispered in prayer as she nursed me back to health, twice—trusting that God would provide what she could not.

Her words echo the promise in Jeremiah 29:11: "For I know the plans I have for you," says the Lord. "They are plans for good and not for disaster, to give you a future and a hope."

I've imagined what those first few days must have been like for my mother when she discovered I had left home. As someone who was always quiet and respectful, my leaving must have shaken her to her core.

Since I shared a room with my brothers, they may have been the first to notice. Maybe one of them woke up and saw the window cracked open, the breeze slipping in where it shouldn't have. I can almost picture them running to tell my parents—my mother calling my name again and again as she moved from room to room, hoping I was just hiding.

My father, checking the yard, looking up and down the road. The chaos. The disbelief. The ache of not knowing. I wasn't there to witness it, but I can feel it now. I can sense how the silence must have settled once they realized I was gone—a silence so heavy it disrupted my mother's peace as she lay awake night after night, tears falling, pleading with God to watch over me.

I don't regret my decision, but I'm not proud of the pain it caused. Unlike how my wife and I raised our children—to speak openly about what was on their minds—no one ever asked me why I left or how. At least, not to me. But I've made peace with that silence, and with many other choices.

I believe my mother's prayers, and the words she spoke over my life when I was young, took root anyway. Over the years, they quietly shaped my decisions more than I realized. That's why I believe you can always go further with God than without Him.

When you show up and give your best, God breathes on it—expanding your reach, increasing your impact, and guiding you toward the people and opportunities you didn't even know you needed. Psalm 116:6 says, "The LORD protects those of childlike faith; I was facing death, and he saved me." I see myself as being the person described in that verse. Many times, I was protected and provided for when I was most vulnerable.

Over the years, I've encountered people and situations I never could have predicted. Some brought more pain than I was prepared for. Still, I take full responsibility. There were times I knew better and could have chosen differently.

Back then, I didn't always see things in terms of right or wrong. I was focused on the freedom to explore. That narrow view came from inexperience and, at times, a refusal to listen to the wisdom being offered.

When you're too focused on yourself, you end up making life harder—not just for you, but for everyone around you—especially when the only voice you trust is your own.

Facing the consequences of my choices eventually taught me to value the lessons I was learning along the way. Those lessons shaped my character and deepened my sense of responsibility to God, to myself, and to others.

I didn't realize I was a teenage runaway until I heard those words spoken back to me while sharing my story. In that moment, I recognized something even greater: God had answered a prayer I didn't even know I needed to pray. And in doing so, He gave me more than safety—He gave me a path, a place, and people who would help shape the man I was becoming.

PAUSE + REFLECT

Provision is more than what's in your hands. It's the unexpected stranger who shows kindness, the doors that open, and the events that defy explanation. It's not just food or a job; it's the courage to take a step forward before clarity comes, and the comfort and grace that meet you when the cost of your choice becomes clear.

Even when you walk away from what's familiar, God walks with you. His plans are already in motion, preparing a future you can only recognize in hindsight.

REFLECTION PROMPTS

- When have you acted on a feeling without a plan, only to see God's provision unfold?

_____

_____

_____

- Who has shown up in your life at just the right time? How might God have sent them?

_____

_____

_____

- How has your view of God's provision changed as you've grown spiritually?

  _____

  _____

  _____

GOD REDIRECTS

WHEN DISRUPTION BECOMES DIRECTION

Your own ears will hear him.
Right behind you a voice will say,
"This is the way you should go,"
whether to the right or to the left.

ISAIAH 30:21

A ROOM AND A NEW RHYTHM

After a bittersweet visit with my parents, I left their home to begin my next chapter, which started with finding a place to stay. Traveling seven miles north, I spotted a small restaurant and motel. I pulled into a parking space in front of the building, walked inside, and hesitated before approaching the first person I saw.

We started talking, and to my surprise, an opportunity quickly emerged. I explained that I was looking for a place to stay but had limited funds. Mrs. Peggy, the owner, suggested we help each other. She needed someone to clean the restaurant in the mornings and wash dishes for a few hours in the evenings.

I paused, not because I was unsure about the offer, but because I had learned to fully understand what's being communicated before committing. She may have read my pause differently. Before I could respond, she leaned in and said, "Some of my patrons tend to get drunk and drop money; you can keep anything you find." I smiled and accepted her offer.

I didn't have much, neither in my pockets nor in my plans. I was just trying to find a place to rest my head. But something about that moment stayed with me. I had spoken honestly about what I needed, listened to what was offered, and made a decision that gave me space to breathe. I knew what I needed, but I did not know where I needed to be. Yet, somehow, I kept ending up in the right place.

I earned about five dollars a day on average, nowhere near enough to support myself and far less than I was used to. After a week at the motel, I started looking for additional work. I remembered a nearby farm where I had once worked with my father, so I stopped by to see if they needed help.

Johnny, the owner, was happy to see me. I didn't say much, nothing about leaving home or where I was staying, but I did tell him about my morning and evening commitments. We agreed I would work from 8 a.m. to 6 p.m.

As summer approached, Johnny needed someone to work from sunrise to sunset and asked if I was interested. While I appreciated Mrs. Peggy's kindness, the discomfort of being around heavy drinkers had started to wear on me. I missed the farm; the calm, quiet rhythm gave me a sense of peace. When I told Mrs. Peggy about my decision, she was understanding and supportive.

The change meant I needed a new place to stay. Johnny mentioned that his labor camp wasn't being used and offered it. Shortly after, he provided a small, one-room trailer. It had no running water or toilet and sat on a patch of land near his house.

I moved in, and in addition to my farm work, I began helping Johnny's wife, Mrs. Anna, with household chores. Twice a month, I also babysat their four children while they attended a Christian event. Their oldest was a thirteen-year-old girl.

Growing up in North Carolina, I had been taught not to make eye contact with White people. I also knew that some believed a Black man could not be trusted alone with a White woman or her children. Because of that, I was surprised—and at first, uncomfortable—by how open and kind this

Italian family from New York was. They treated me like one of their own, and I even stopped calling Johnny "Mister."

Mrs. Anna often checked on me. "Willie, how are you doing? Is Johnny treating you right?" she would ask with a laugh. "He tries to work everybody to death." I appreciated her concern, but the truth was I enjoyed working for Johnny and living on the farm.

BREAKING THE PLOW—AND THE PATTERN

I'll never forget the moment I fully realized Mrs. Anna's sincerity.

It was a sunny autumn day, and I was plowing the land in preparation for next year's harvest. I rode the tractor with the newly attached rollover plow. Although I had used it before, the loud crash it made when flipping still startled me every time I turned.

I must have been distracted, because as I made a turn, I forgot to slow down. The plow slammed into the ground, and cracked in several places. When I looked back and saw the damage, a wave of panic rushed over me. What had I done?

Hearing the bang, Johnny ran over to see what had happened. He approached with a stern expression and then began yelling—angrier than I had ever seen him. I froze, feeling helpless, like a child wanting to escape a parent's fury but with nowhere to go.

What we now call "triggered" is exactly what I experienced—an intense emotional reaction when a present experience stirs up an old trauma. For me, feeling disrespected is one of those triggers. In that moment, anger started to rise. I stepped off the tractor.

Hearing the commotion, Mrs. Anna came outside. As she walked toward us, she called out calmly, "Johnny, what's going on out here?"

Before he could answer, I jumped in. "Mrs. Anna, I'll tell you what's going on. I broke the plow. I understand he's upset, but I won't stand for him screaming at me."

Her response was immediate—and protective. "Johnny, you know better than to talk to Willie like that."

It felt like she was standing up for me, reminding him, and maybe even me, of the respect we all deserve. As she spoke, I could feel the tension begin to lift.

Then she added, "If Willie needs to learn something, teach him. If he can't handle it, find him something else to do."

When she finished speaking, she turned and walked back into the house. No one said another word. Johnny made a call to get the plow repaired, and I busied myself with other tasks around the farm.

Once the plow was fixed, Johnny took the time to train me properly.

Looking back, Mrs. Anna's kindness, wisdom, and motherly strength reminded me of God's presence. Her actions that day became a powerful lesson in respect, understanding, and the importance of managing my emotions—a skill that has taken years to develop.

Writing this book has helped me see what was truly happening in that moment. It was never just about a broken plow; it was about something buried much deeper.

BURIED BUT NOT GONE

I was eight years old when my father took my brother and me to New York for work. One Sunday afternoon, he told me to get in the truck. After a short drive, we arrived at another labor camp nearby. It didn't look familiar, and I wasn't sure if I had ever been there before.

During the ride, my father didn't seem upset. But when the truck stopped, he reached for his gun, which sat on top of the heater on the passenger side, just below the dashboard. Before opening the door, he looked at me and said, "Stay in the truck."

A few moments later, I heard commotion and peeked over the dashboard. I saw a line of people coming out of a building with their hands raised. At the end of the line was my father, gun in hand, instructing them to turn and face the building.

Once everyone was against the wall, he walked back to the truck, placed the gun on the heater, and drove off. To this day, I still don't know what happened. But about ten minutes later, we were pulled over by the police.

I looked in the side-view mirror and saw the officers step out of their car and head toward us. When they were about halfway to the driver's side, one of them cocked his shotgun. That sharp, metallic sound—part pump, part snap—echoed through the street and lodged in my memory.

That sound didn't live in the past; it lived in me. Nine years later, at seventeen, when the plow slammed into the ground, I reacted without thinking. Now, at eighty-five, I can see it clearly: the sound of that plow had triggered a moment I had never processed—a sound I had carried for decades without realizing it.

This is what I know now: the past doesn't leave us. It waits to be acknowledged, understood, and healed.

BURNED BY THE LIE

I still had—and still have—a lot to learn about unprocessed emotions and the way past experiences shape our decisions. This happened just a few months after the plow incident, and this time, I could have been seriously injured or even killed. I am thankful for God's protection, guidance, and mercy.

I earned $58 a week, regardless of the job. In the winter, when there was no planting or harvesting, I cut down trees to help clear the land. We burned the branches and debris to save on disposal costs.

Johnny always started the fires. I watched closely as he soaked the branches in gasoline, stepped back, lit a piece of paper, and tossed it into the pile. That day—like every other day before he headed to Mrs. Peggy's restaurant—he reminded me, "No matter what the fire looks like, don't pour gasoline on it once it's lit. Do not bother with the gasoline."

After I added more debris to the fire, the flames began to fade, producing only smoke. Thinking I could speed things up, I decided to take matters into my own hands. Instead of following the usual process—pouring the gasoline into the smaller can and sprinkling it on the pile—I grabbed the gas can, stepped back, and threw it directly onto the dying flames.

A fire erupted, and my eyes locked onto the surge of red and orange as the flames leapt into the air. The heat slammed into my body, and within seconds, my face began to burn. I was terrified.

My first instinct was to run, but instead, I threw myself into a nearby snowbank, desperate to extinguish the flames.

For the next month, my face stung with pain, the burns leaving behind faint scars. I applied Vaseline every day to soothe the raw skin. The fire had singed off my eyebrows, and they never grew back.

Ashamed of what I'd done, I kept it to myself. I was relieved that Johnny didn't seem to notice my blistered skin or question the change in my face.

But from that day forward, I carried something more than physical scars. I learned a lasting lesson: just because you disagree with someone doesn't mean they're out to harm you.

Looking back, here's what I believe happened. Despite the trust Johnny and I had built over months of working together, something shifted after the plow incident. I began telling myself a new story—one rooted not in truth, but in fear—about who he was and how he felt about me.

When he warned me about the gasoline, I didn't hear concern; I heard control. In my mind, he wasn't protecting me; he was just trying to save himself a few dollars. Pride and unresolved pain twisted his caution into something it wasn't.

How many times have you argued with someone about one thing, only to convince yourself they no longer love you, care about you, or are simply using you for their own benefit?

That day changed something in me. I became more open to advice from older people, even when I didn't fully understand what they were saying or why it mattered. Pain has a way of clarifying what pride refuses to see: wisdom, often wrapped in words we are not quite ready to receive.

Sometimes, a person's guidance truly does come from care and lived experience. But if we are not careful, we will rewrite their wisdom as insult, buy into a lie, and pay a price we can't afford.

I paid a small price for a big lesson, and only because God's presence, provision, and protection were with me. For that, I am deeply grateful.

SILVER WISDOM FROM 1890

The longer I worked for Johnny, the closer our relationship became, and that bond soon extended to his father and other family members. Johnny's father owned a farm in Long Island, and whenever he needed help, Johnny and I would go to lend a hand.

While we were there, they set up living quarters for me away from the labor camp. No matter where we went, I always felt like part of their family.

I vividly remember Johnny's older brother. He walked with a cane after having a stroke, but he never let that stop him from visiting. He'd come by just to talk, sharing stories about life, his time in the city, and the lessons he'd learned the hard way. I didn't say much; I just listened.

He moved slowly, but his presence was steady, and his words even more so.

The day before I left, he handed me my first silver coin and said, "If you don't spend this, you'll never be broke."

It was more than money; it symbolized our friendship—his way of saying, "I'm with you. I want what's good for you." That coin wasn't just currency. It was a quiet inheritance of respect, trust, and a lesson in what truly lasts.

I still have that coin—and his words—to this day.

THE CALL OF THE CROWD

With little to do, I often visited juke joints to people-watch during my downtime. The bars buzzed with loud music, swinging dancers, and plenty of drinks.

Fights occasionally broke out, and judging by how close some patrons were, it was clear that more than dancing was on their minds.

I sat alone, unconcerned with what others were doing, just passing time and trying to understand life. Suddenly, I heard my name called out in the noisy atmosphere.

"Bill!"

I turned and looked around.

Again—"Bill!"

A childhood classmate emerged from the crowd, surrounded by a group of men. I recognized a few of their faces, but one stood out immediately: Side-Eyed Sam. They called him that not because he was shady, but because one of his eyes wandered while the other seemed to look straight through you.

My first thought was, *Oh no*. I had never been comfortable in crowds, even familiar ones, but I was gracious. Some grabbed chairs and scooted up to my table while others stood nearby. We laughed and reminisced about growing up in North Carolina. Then someone brought up the fight I had with Side-Eyed Sam on my last day of school.

"Man, remember when you knocked the wind out of him?" someone said, grinning.

Laughter circled the table. Side-Eyed Sam had been huge back then. Now, with him towering over me, the fear returned. I didn't want to fight him then, and I didn't want to fight him now.

They moved on quickly, but I didn't. From the moment I saw him, my mind went back to when I was seven years old. I remembered it vividly: a circle of grown men placing bets on kids fighting. I was small and frightened as my uncle's voice urged me to step into a makeshift ring.

I walked into the circle, clenched my fists, and with a rush of adrenaline, shoved him hard, knocking the wind out of him. Then I ran straight back to the classroom. Only when I stopped did I realize what I had done. I was shaking, hoping I would never see him again.

And now, here I was, sitting at a table with the same group, laughing at stories I wished had stayed buried. I didn't want to talk about the fight, but they did. Still, there was no tension, no revenge—and I was relieved.

It was a friendly evening that ended with an invitation to join them for future adventures. I knew deep down it wasn't a good idea. I had always kept to myself and saw no appeal in hanging out with men who drank and fought, but I went anyway.

Each outing made me feel tougher, like I was the man in charge. I began to enjoy the edge it gave me. I started to take pride in the hard life, in the toughness it demanded. My buddies fueled that feeling, treating me like the big man, untouchable. Around them, I was somebody.

The problem was I had to prove myself constantly to keep my status growing, and what was expected of me became increasingly extreme. Even as a teen, I had the strength of a grown man and could make older guys back down from me and my friends.

Unlike the quiet respect I had earned on the farm, this was adrenaline-driven power—instant, fleeting, and addictive. On a deeper level, the freedom to express bottled-up emotions was also a key part of my enjoyment and acceptance of being on the street. Still, I noticed a change in my thinking as I saw people getting hurt.

I asked myself, *Am I going to get hurt like my buddy?* That was when I realized I needed to distance myself from that crowd. The conversations I had with myself about the dangers of this path grew sharper and louder.

I knew that drinking and fighting, whether with others or sometimes among ourselves, would lead to more serious consequences—like jail or worse. Have you ever been with the wrong crowd, feeling like nothing good could come from it?

I should have informed everyone before I disappeared, but like leaving home, I just slipped away. It often felt easier not to share my plans because whenever I did, someone tried to convince me I was wrong.

I learned early that I had to trust myself and be willing to accept the consequences of my choices. I stayed away from the juke joints until Johnny and I went back to Delaware.

All those distractions—the wrong crowds, unprocessed fear, and hollow attention—shaped a new resolve in me. After that, I kept my distance. Some places and people don't deserve a second visit.

QUIET REFLECTION, NEW RESOLVE

With so much time alone, I reflected on the streets I had walked, the people I had met, and the choices I was making.

I thought deeply about what I wanted to escape, and why it was important to leave it behind. I wrestled with wanting to avoid drinking while still going to places where it was common—and with all the trouble that came with it.

Even though I wasn't fully aware of it at the time, God was already showing me another way—through kindness, care, and honest work. Johnny's family didn't just offer me a place to stay; they offered me a different way to live.

Every gesture was a balm to my tired spirit, reminding me that kindness still exists in the world. Deep down, I sensed that I, too, could have a better life.

Just as I had done before running away from home, I sat alone and considered what it would take to build something more stable. I concluded that marriage was the answer—a chance at stability and a fresh start. I wasn't sure where that thought came from or why I believed it so strongly, but I remember telling myself, *William, you're going back to Delaware, and you're going to marry somebody's daughter.* And that's exactly what I did.

PAUSE + REFLECT

God doesn't need your permission to protect you. Sometimes, His redirection comes quietly—through people, tension, or a growing discomfort that whispers, "It's time to move on." Other times, it's a deep, silent knowing that you no longer belong where you are.

What feels like disruption is often divine direction. When you look back, you may see that breaking a promise, ignoring good advice, or flirting with danger became part of God's guidance—not as punishment or rejection, but as a gentle nudge toward a better path.

REFLECTION PROMPTS

- When a past wound surfaces unexpectedly, do you treat it as a setback or a signal? How might God be inviting you to look deeper?

_____

_____

_____

- Have you ever resisted a change, only to realize it was the redirection you needed?

_____

_____

- How did you recognize the right path when the road felt uncertain?

CHAPTER 2

FINDING ALIGNMENT WITH GOD

GOD KNOWS THE PATH; PEACE REVEALS IT

I know, Lord, that our lives are not our own.
We are not able to plan our own course.

JEREMIAH 10:23

S. RENEE'S MOMENTS TO MEASURE

CHAPTER 2

When life feels off course, it's not always punishment; it could be preparation. What feels like confusion or discomfort might be divine guidance nudging you toward alignment. If you pause and reflect, you may begin to see that purpose often starts to take shape when life feels most uncertain.

Finding Alignment with God invites you to explore how He uses emotional pressure, misunderstanding, and even your uncertainty to shape you for His purpose.

In Lessons 4–6, you'll discover:

- When you feel unready, God is already working through your desire to grow.

- You might be misunderstood, but God knows what others cannot see.

- The pressure you feel today is shaping your capacity for tomorrow.

- Surrender often transforms survival into meaning.

SEEKING A REASON

FEELING MY WAY FORWARD

We can make our plans, but the Lord determines our steps.

PROVERBS 16:9

THE LACK OF KNOWLEDGE

For as long as I can remember, I've had conversations with myself. They were simple thoughts that often raised questions without easy answers. I would ask, "What's the next step?" and "When will you act?" Over time, those talks became a warning: take hold of your life, or life will take hold of you.

I thought marriage would be my salvation, but I hadn't fully considered the weight of that decision. It was selfish to ask someone to entrust their life to me when I hadn't yet figured out my own. I didn't know what she could expect from me—or even what I expected of myself. Looking back, I see how unexamined choices can lead to unexpected consequences far beyond what we imagine, not only for us but also for those we pull into our uncertainty.

But before I made that decision—who to marry—there was a moment of stillness I didn't expect.

A woman walked down the street, and I found myself captivated, wondering who she was and where she was headed. Her beauty drew me in, but it was the elegance and quiet confidence in her steps that truly intrigued me.

As she faded from view, I stood frozen, unable to call out to her, and she never knew I was there. Yet it wasn't long before I saw her again.

BACK TO SCHOOL—
BUT NOT BACK ON TRACK

Although I disliked school, I saw it as a necessary step to go further in life. At seventeen, despite my hesitation, I re-enrolled and picked up where I had left off in ninth grade. My classmates were only thirteen or fourteen. I was stronger than most boys, but my small frame helped me blend in.

It didn't take long to realize how steep the challenges were. The greatest was my lack of basic reading and writing skills. Back then, I would have been labeled illiterate; today, they would diagnose me with a learning disability. Yet neither word fully captures my story—or the potential within me.

What made returning to school so difficult wasn't only the academics; it was the weight of everything that came before. To understand that moment, you would have to know how far behind I already was, and why.

A FAILED SYSTEM

My father was a crew boss for migrant workers. I started working at age seven, traveling with my family across the country in the back of trucks to reach farms where we were scheduled to work. That meant I missed a lot of school, unless the state sent social workers to labor camps to report violations of labor laws. That didn't happen often; I recall it only once, in Buffalo, New York.

Back then, I was still at home. My younger sister, Alice, often helped me with my homework—usually completing it for me. I let her; I didn't know how to do it myself.

My English teacher asked, "How can you earn A's on homework and fail every test?"

I replied, "I don't know."

She compassionately assumed I was tired from working, but she had no idea how much was happening in my life.

After my mother became seriously ill, we stopped traveling. That's when we settled in Delaware—and that season changed everything. My older siblings and I took on more responsibility. I helped care for the family, and school became secondary.

Years later, when I returned to school on my own, those old struggles came back. The gaps were still there—maybe even larger. The shame I felt in not knowing how to read or write hadn't gone anywhere. When problems go unaddressed, they don't disappear; they impact more areas of your life, waiting for you to recognize and address them.

HIDING WHAT I COULDN'T UNDERSTAND

When I returned to school, I was determined to push through, but my continued struggle with understanding the fundamentals created an inner tension I couldn't shake. One teacher tried to help me catch up, but my inability to grasp the material wore her patience thin. Frustrated, she said, "You are the stupidest boy I have ever seen!"

That moment stuck with me. It wasn't just the words—it was what I already feared: that I didn't belong, and maybe never would. Rather than motivating me, the experience made me want to disappear.

My feelings of inadequacy only intensified my desire to escape what felt like a stifling environment. After just two months, I dropped out again, overwhelmed by the pressure and unaware of what I truly needed.

Isn't that how we often react to pressure? We push it away. We blame others. We walk out rather than looking inward to address what we don't understand about ourselves.

I didn't realize it at the time, but even in my frustration and failure, God was planting something. I was navigating the delicate space between vulnerability and resilience, and I didn't yet know that both could coexist.

Maybe it was that tension that fueled my hope that marriage would bring stability. But marriage, I've learned, doesn't fix what hasn't been faced. It requires emotional readiness and the right tools to build something lasting.

Still, even then, God's plan was unfolding. As Proverbs 16:9 says, "We can make our plans, but the Lord determines our steps." Slowly, I was growing, and He was shaping me within it.

FINDING A REASON

I didn't go far in school. I struggled to shake the feelings of being lost, voiceless, and unsure of where I belonged. That's when I saw her—the mystery girl.

She became a steady light in my life, her presence giving me a sense of direction amid my confusion. Looking back, I believe it was with her that I first found a reason to keep going.

PAUSE + REFLECT

Sometimes, you move forward without knowing why—driven by pressure, pain, or the quiet hope that something will eventually make sense. Looking back, you may discover that, even in your confusion, you were being shaped.

The steps that once seemed aimless were actually laying the groundwork— a seed of clarity, a glimpse of purpose, a path that becomes visible only in hindsight.

God is always present. You don't always listen to His guidance, but He is never surprised by your choices. Even your missteps can be part of His plan.

REFLECTION PROMPTS

- What are your internal conversations revealing about your current situation?

  _____

  _____

  _____

- When the path ahead felt unclear, what signals helped you recognize the right next step?

  _____

  _____

  _____

- What has unexpected redirection taught you about who you are and how God works in the gaps?

  _____

  _____

  _____

LOST IN THE MIDDLE
THE BATTLE BETWEEN
CHAOS AND CALLING

Don't judge by his appearance or height, for I have rejected him.
The Lord doesn't see things the way you see them.
People judge by outward appearance, but the Lord looks at the heart.

1 SAMUEL 16:7

TOO SOON TO SEE IT

In those few months back in school, unexpected moments—some confusing, others revealing—began pushing me toward a decision that would change everything.

One day, after finishing my shift in the potato field, I was still in my dusty work clothes when a group of guys from school noticed my car parked in the field at the farm. They pulled over and called out, "Bill, come ride with us to Smyrna."

I assumed we were just going for a drive, but to my surprise, we ended up at a dance. When they said they were going inside, I shook my head and replied, "I'm not going in looking like this. I'll stay in the car until you come back."

A few minutes later, they returned with a girl beside them. We exchanged glances as they walked up to the car to introduce us. From her expression, I could see both curiosity and confusion, as if she were silently asking, *Why are you introducing me to him?*

Neither of us said a word. She looked at me, then turned and walked back into the hall. I sat in the car, unsettled. Something about it felt strangely personal, but I couldn't explain why. Was it because I was with "the boys," and her reaction felt like rejection? Or maybe I was just lost in my own thoughts: *What's going on? Why did they bring me here without saying anything?* Then again, maybe I should have asked where we were headed.

Then it hit me: she was the same girl I had seen walking down the street just a few days earlier. I still don't know if the guys brought me there to introduce us, but if that was the plan, it didn't make much sense.

Later, one of the guys told me she had asked, "Why would I want to meet him?" It stung, but looking back, I have learned this: no experience is wasted, even the ones that make no sense at the time. They often connect to something bigger—a lesson, a pattern, or a piece of the vision we are still growing into.

When I first heard her question, I thought she was arrogant. But it wasn't long before I saw more in her decision. She had standards, and I have come to respect people who know what matters to them and stand by it.

Months later, I saw her again at school. She was in the middle of an argument with another female classmate.

I didn't know what it was about, but I jumped in and said to the thirteen-year-old, "Why are you always bothering people? Why don't you leave her alone?"

I'm not even sure why I said anything, it was so unlike me. I usually followed my father's advice: "Each year you have six months to leave other people's business alone and six months to pay attention to your own business." Put simply, in today's language, he was telling me to stay in my lane.

Maybe, on a subconscious level, I felt disappointed by her rejection and wanted to strike back. Or maybe I hadn't yet learned how to recognize, express, and manage my emotions, and deep down, I craved her attention. Either way, she swung at me.

She has her version of what happened, but in my memory, I was grabbing her by the wrists to keep her from hitting me in the face. Hearing the commotion, our science teacher, Mr. Grant, rushed into the classroom and stood between us to separate us. Once things were calm, he walked us both to the principal's office.

As we walked down the hall, Mr. Grant said firmly, "William, I know your parents. I'm surprised at you."

Then driving home a sharper point, he sarcastically added, "I didn't know you were into fighting girls."

My voice rose an octave as I explained, "I wasn't hitting her. I was trying to keep her from hitting me in the face. That's all I was doing."

Of course, she went silent, maybe thinking the same thing I was: *What the heck just happened?*

After that incident, we spoke but didn't have much more to say to each other. That was, until there was a reason for us to disagree again.

THE RUMOR AND MY EGO

During school hours each year, the administration allowed students to walk to the nearby theater to watch a movie. On my way, I passed a tall, muscular female student who struck up a conversation with me.

When we arrived at the theater, I sat beside her to continue our discussion. After the film ended, I walked with her back to school. I thought it was an innocent exchange, but a rumor soon started: she was my girlfriend.

Who would spread a rumor about me? I wondered. I went through a mental list of classmates, trying to figure out who was responsible. I settled on the mystery girl.

It's strange how quickly gossip finds a foothold. I kept asking myself, *Why did her rejection stick with me? Was it pride? Curiosity? Fascination? Jealousy? Did she start the rumor, or did I blame her just to have a reason to connect with her?*

That's what rumors do; they remind you that you can't control how others tell your story. They can make you feel powerless, forcing you to spend time chasing them—trying to reclaim the narrative, hoping to rewrite it in your favor.

What I learned from this, and similar situations, was that I shouldn't waste energy worrying about what others think of me. It's my story, and how I choose to live my life each day gives me the power to shape it.

I never found out who started the rumor, and I didn't care. During my final three weeks, the mystery girl and I started talking. The more we talked, the more we discovered how much we had in common, which soon led to invitations to visit her at her home.

Her mother welcomed me warmly, and before long, our visits became frequent. We realized our family dynamics and life experiences reflected each other in surprising ways. We built a close friendship—it felt like a divine bond that had always been there, just waiting for us to recognize it.

We were young and fragile then, struggling to understand and align our actions with our feelings. We expended a lot of energy protecting ourselves. Although we recognized the consequences of this early in our relationship and have grown since, we still haven't mastered being vulnerable and leaning into our spiritual strengths to ease moments of tension.

STILL BECOMING

I've come to believe that it's in navigating these complexities that relationships truly take shape, and that buried pain rises to the surface. They stir love and frustration, joy and grief, hope and disappointment, sometimes all at once. When we feel these emotions, we come to understand and see the delicate balance between connection and neglect.

I couldn't see it at the time, but the chaos was a calling. In the midst of misunderstandings, missteps, and even the mystery girl, God was reshaping not just how I saw her—but how I saw myself.

PAUSE + REFLECT

Things rarely make sense when you're caught in the middle. The truth is hard to explain; your intentions get misunderstood, and sometimes, even you don't know exactly what you're feeling.

But God sees beyond the confusion. He hears what you truly mean, not just what you say. He stays close, patiently guiding you toward clarity, growth, and a deeper love.

REFLECTION PROMPTS

- Can you recall a time you felt misjudged or misunderstood? What did you learn about yourself through it?

  _____

  _____

  _____

- What is the tension between the image you present and your internal conflict?

  _____

  _____

  _____

- What part of your story are you still carrying that keeps you "lost in the middle"? How might God be inviting clarity?

_____

_____

_____

PURPOSE TRANSFORMS REASON

WHEN SURVIVAL BECOMES SURRENDER

The thief's purpose is to steal and kill and destroy.
My purpose is to give them a rich and satisfying life.

JOHN 10:10

GOD WAS IN IT ALL

The mystery girl was Shirley M. Taylor—not just a fleeting figure in my story, but, over time, a defining part of it.

Confident, beautiful, and poised, she moved with purpose. A majorette dreaming of becoming a nurse, she already had her sights set on college and pictured herself married with six children. I'll admit I was drawn to her shapeliness, but it was her commanding presence, inner resilience, and clear vision for her life that truly captured me.

I felt fortunate to have her in my life. But to some—including teachers who recognized her potential—I was a nobody: a high school dropout, a potato picker with no visible path to success. They warned her to stay away from me, implying I could keep her from a prosperous future. Yet from the moment I met her, Shirley proved she was an independent thinker, making choices that aligned with her own values.

We dated for three years. During that time, she cleaned houses and attended school while I worked on the farm. We married after she completed the eleventh grade, just twenty days after her seventeenth birthday; I was twenty. Our plan was for Shirl, as I call her, to return to school in the fall and finish twelfth grade.

Until then, I lived alone in a one-room trailer about ten feet wide and thirty feet long, with no indoor bathroom or running water. It belonged to the farmer and sat on his property. None of this bothered me at the time—I was responsible only for myself and had little vision for anything more.

But after we married, I realized what I had overlooked: my wife's needs were different. Going outside to use the bathroom, hauling water in buckets, and keeping enough in the tub for a bath became more than an inconvenience. My perspective began to shift, and for the first time, I felt the full weight of being a husband.

To ease my sense of inadequacy, I rigged a hose to supply water to the trailer, but it still wasn't enough. Each day, the reality of our situation pressed harder, reminding me I needed to think beyond myself. She deserved a safe, comfortable home that met her needs and supported her well-being.

Then there was the $100 we borrowed from a teacher when we married. Before its due date, he asked for repayment, and that moment taught me something: I never wanted to be in a position where I had to borrow from others to care for my family. More than anything, I didn't want my wife to be ashamed of who I was or what I could provide.

These external struggles were only a glimpse of the battle I was fighting inside.

A PROMISE I WASN'T SURE I COULD KEEP

Shortly after we got married, Shirl told me she was pregnant. Looking into her eyes and hearing that news awakened something deep inside me. I knew I had to find a way to keep my promise to her and our unborn child.

Within a few weeks, our lives began changing quickly, and my responsibilities grew steadily. I had dropped out of school a few years earlier, and now she was pregnant and could not go back—something we were excited about but had not considered before we married.

Fear began to set in. Going through life alone was easy. Usually, dealing with others left me in silence, wanting to run away. This wasn't like before. Day and night, I wrestled with how to improve our lives. Though I wasn't sure what "better" looked like, I became obsessed with figuring it out. One day at work, I was driving the tractor in the field when I was overcome with emotion. The weight of my responsibilities pressed heavily on my chest.

In that moment, I felt a deep sense of humility and vulnerability. I needed help—more than I could give myself and more than anyone else could offer.

I had made a promise to her that I wasn't sure I could keep, yet I felt a strong urge to honor my commitment to her and to our child. I owed them the best life I could provide. I knew I was a hard worker, but I also knew I lacked education. I could not do it alone.

The wisdom my mother shared, which went beyond her formal education, and the unwavering faith that helped her overcome a life-threatening illness, ultimately inspired me to call on Jesus for myself. Whenever I needed help, I followed my mother's advice: "If you are ever in trouble, call on Jesus, and He will hear you."

GOD BRINGS THE INCREASE

Throughout my short life, I had faced many situations where my mother's advice proved helpful. This time was different. There were no empty promises and no bargaining with God. I wasn't trying to avoid trouble. I was finally on the right track, and I needed real help.

Surrounded by the stillness of the fields, I was completely open to an answer. The burden I carried demanded more than just a way to survive; it called for surrender.

My mind drifted back to the days when my mother took my siblings and me to church. I rarely understood the meaning behind the choir's songs or the preacher's message, and I couldn't understand why people were moved to "get in the spirit."

Shirl and I were in church every Sunday, but I was just sitting in the pew, unmoved and unchanged. Still, those moments had left an impression on me. Even though I hadn't fully understood them at the time, they had taken root. Now, in my desperation, the teachings about faith and trusting God began to resurface, igniting a spark of hope I hadn't realized I needed.

A CRY FROM THE FIELD

That day, at twenty-one years old, while riding the tractor, tears streamed down my cheeks—grief, hope, fear, and wonderment all spilling out at once. I stopped the tractor, climbed down, and walked through the crops, needing to breathe, to feel.

The sun warmed my skin, and the earthy scent of the field engulfed me. Then, without warning, an indescribable feeling washed over me. It was as if I were being consumed by a force that was too vast to be contained, yet undeniably alive within me. In that moment, I felt lifted—cradled in the arms of unconditional love.

Suddenly, I was screaming uncontrollably, releasing emotions I did not know I was holding. I needed the courage and capacity to go further, and I knew this was it. Right then, I accepted Christ as my personal Savior.

I may never fully understand what God intended when He touched me that day, but I know it was a moment of divine significance. And maybe not everything awakened that day can be fully understood, grasped, or used. However, as a former farmer, the sacred and physical work of sowing seeds, nurturing growth, and bringing in a harvest is understood.

After accepting Christ, I didn't ask for anything extraordinary. I didn't pray for a big house or a lot of money. I didn't ask for people to know my name. Instead, I asked God for the strength to do whatever was necessary—within the limits of the law—to care for those who depended on me.

More than anything, I feared disappointing my family. My prayer was simple: "God, help me care for my family." That day, my resolve was strengthened. I made an unshakable commitment, with every fiber of my being, to rise to the occasion and face whatever lies ahead with faith—giving up was not an option.

That moment didn't solve all my problems, but it changed the way I carried them.

PAUSE + REFLECT

What if the moments when you feel most overwhelmed are actually when God is activating what He has already placed inside you?

You may be facing a challenge and searching for answers, but God could be leading you toward something not even on your radar yet. Even if His plan isn't clear to you, the first step is shifting from a mindset of fear and doubt to one rooted in trust and centered on Him.

You carry what you believe you must, but when you release it to God, everything changes. He doesn't just lighten the load—He transforms it. That's when life begins to feel full. Not perfect, but purposeful.

REFLECTION PROMPTS

- Can you recall a moment when simply trying to survive led you to something deeper? What shifted in you?

- Are you more focused on God's purpose or the blessing you hope it brings?

- What would you have to do to surrender your timeline, your plans, and ask God to realign you with His purpose?

  _____

  _____

  _____

CHAPTER 3

PROVISION
FOR PURPOSE
PROVISION IN FAILED PLANS

And we know that God causes everything to work
together for the good of those who love God and
are called according to his purpose for them.

ROMANS 8:28

S. RENEE'S MOMENTS TO MEASURE

CHAPTER 3

Provision doesn't always look like progress. Sometimes, it starts with a closed door, a delayed plan, or an unexpected detour. But if you keep moving forward, you'll often discover that what seems like a setback is a divine setup.

Provision for Purpose encourages you to discover how grace, grit, and belief come together to light the way God has prepared, even when you're unsure of where it leads.

In Lessons 7–9, you'll realize:

- A closed door isn't rejection; it's redirection.

- The right path seldom begins with clarity; it usually starts with courage.

- When you trust God enough to take action, He will meet you in motion.

- Faith grows through risk, resilience, and resolve.

GOING BACK TO GO FURTHER

WORK, WORTH, AND THE WHISPER OF GOD

The Lord directs the steps of the godly.
He delights in every detail of their lives.
Though they stumble, they will never fall,
for the Lord holds them by the hand.

PSALM 37:23-24

GOD'S UNRECOGNIZED CLUE

Johnny and Mrs. Anna weren't wealthy farm owners, but they gave me something priceless that shaped my outlook: a sense of family. Still, I knew that if we were going to live better, I had to improve our financial situation, so I asked Johnny for a raise.

As I suspected, he couldn't pay me more. Instead, he offered me a piece of unused land on his property where I could grow crops. I was free to plant whatever I wanted, and he would provide the seeds and fertilizer upfront. At the end of the year, he would sell the harvest, subtract his costs, and give me the remaining profit. I could work on my "side hustle" after working hours.

At the time, I didn't realize I was entering into a sharecropping arrangement—a practice with deep historical roots dating back to the slavery era.

After the Civil War, many formerly enslaved people lacked resources or land.

Sharecropping became a system that allowed them to farm in exchange for a portion of the crops or other resources. Tragically, this often led to cycles of debt and poverty, as landowners retained control over their workers' livelihoods.

Reflecting on it now, I believe this was God's way of introducing me to entrepreneurship. I always thought my first business was pouring concrete, but now I see it actually started on the farm.

Have you ever missed God's signs? Maybe you were too focused on what you thought others were doing to you and overlooked what God was doing for you.

This reminds me of John 3:8, where Jesus says, "The wind blows wherever it wants. Just as you can hear the wind but can't tell where it comes from or where it is going, so you can't explain how people are born of the Spirit."

When things look unfair, it's easy to think God's not in it. In John 13:7, Jesus tells us, "You don't understand now what I am doing, but someday you will."

On the surface, it looked like I was being denied. I asked for more money and got more work. The truth is this: the "raise" didn't come in dollars; it came in development. God was building my character to handle the blessing I didn't yet know was coming.

WISDOM WAITING

I chose cauliflower because I thought it would be one of the easiest vegetables to grow. I quickly learned it wasn't. To keep the cauliflower heads white, we had to tie the leaves around them to shield them from sunlight.

Shirl was well into her pregnancy and worked alongside me in the field during the evenings. Even though she never complained, it hurt to see her bent over with her belly pressing against the plants as she carefully tied the leaves.

Her dedication reminded me that she wasn't getting a fair deal, and that I owed her better. Still, we did what we had to do together. And our bond grew stronger—not through grand moments or public celebrations, but through shared sacrifice.

Even so, I kept asking myself, *How could I become a better provider?*

The year we were married and the one that followed brought the harsh winters of 1960 and 1961, bitter cold winds and freezing temperatures that threatened the crops. The weather had a direct impact on the potatoes I grew for the farmer, and although he found temporary work for me, it wasn't sustainable.

The severe weather and crop loss made it impossible for my boss to pay me. When he told me he had to let me go, I believed everything would work out, but I couldn't ignore the fact that I had a family to feed. I needed to find another job quickly.

The toughest part was telling Shirl I had lost my job. She had recently given birth to our son, and I didn't want to let her down. But she surprised me. In just six months, she had saved almost $300, and I was deeply grateful.

From the beginning, I was learning something vital about the woman I had married: she wasn't the type to waste money or lead us into debt, distraction, or despair. I'd bring home the money, give it to her, and she'd buy what we needed and save the rest. The only time I ever objected to Shirl buying something on credit was when she purchased a television. It wasn't expensive, just a basic model. We watched it together that night, and the next morning I told her, "Take it back and put every penny back into the account." She didn't explain why she bought it, argue, or even ask for an explanation. She just returned it.

But I now see that I didn't handle it the right way. While I still believe it was a sound financial decision that set us on a path of discipline and good money management, I never asked her why the television mattered to her. I made a decision that directly affected her without first having a conversation.

1 Peter 3:7 advises, "In the same way, you husbands must give honor to your wives. Treat your wife with understanding as you live together." I didn't take the time to understand—not because I didn't care, but because I didn't know how. I acted based on my past, not on our partnership.

Looking back, she was home each day with small children and the responsibilities of running a household. The television might have offered her mental stimulation, companionship, or simply a way to stay connected to the outside world.

If I knew then what I know now about relationships, I would have told her this:

> When I was single, I made a foolish choice. I got paid on Friday, and by Sunday night, my pockets were empty. I'd partied all weekend, not thinking about the week ahead. And when I reached for my lunch money that evening, there was nothing left. Just the realization that I had spent it all—with nothing to show for it but regret.
>
> I was too ashamed to ask for a loan. I thought: *William, if you're foolish enough to spend every dime you have, then you'll face the consequences.* That week, I scraped together whatever food I could find to silence the empty, nagging growl in my stomach. And I promised myself I would save a portion of every paycheck and never live beyond my means again.
>
> I had already paid the price once, and I refused to let my family suffer the consequences of a lesson I'd already learned.

If I could go back, I would sit with her and say, "Help me understand what you need," because understanding is more valuable than any boundary we think we are protecting. Proverbs 4:7 reminds us, "Getting wisdom is the wisest thing you can do! And whatever else you do, develop good judgment." I now know that good judgment begins with understanding.

What's remarkable is that she didn't just accept the situation; she transformed it. Her response became a principle we've followed throughout our lives. Even though I failed to recognize what she needed in that moment, she not only honored it with grace but also understood its deeper meaning.

HELPED—NOT HEALED

I enjoyed living on the farm. Watching things grow was incredibly satisfying, and if the business's success hadn't depended on uncontrollable factors like the weather, I might be a retired farmer.

But we have our plans, and God has His. The choice is always ours: follow what we see or trust where He leads. I prayed to support my family, and God answered—but not in the way I expected.

What if the answer to your prayer wasn't God opening a door, but you becoming someone who no longer needed that door?

I thought He would help me with the work I was doing. Instead, He opened a different door and led me into a new profession. We pray for outcomes, but God shows us the way—and it's often the one we never would have chosen on our own.

That's not because God is trying to trick us, but because He knows what He's placed inside us and what it will take to draw it out. He sees the full picture: what we desire, what we need, and the path that will lead us there.

I immediately started searching for a job, and our savings helped ease the stress of the situation. Hoping to find work, I decided to visit my father, who owned a construction business. I was sure he was hiring and thought I could help, even though I knew nothing about the industry.

He offered to pay me $100 a week, almost twice what I had earned on the farm. I was grateful and excited, promising to do my best.

I learned how to pour concrete and build steps. My father, who called me Bill, was impressed by my work ethic and how quickly I caught on. Within a few days, he assigned me a team and had me leading a jobsite.

Everything seemed perfect—until I realized I had overlooked a crucial detail: we hadn't discussed how many hours I would need to work to earn that $100 a week. That was my fault. When we first spoke about the job, I never asked what his expectations were.

My dad had a way of pushing you until you almost passed out, then telling you to get up, drink some water, and keep going. It didn't take long for

me to realize that he expected me to work all day and stay late to finish paperwork. As a result, I often worked nearly twenty hours a day, six days a week.

I didn't know my father's full story, but I did know this: he was strong-
willed, had little tolerance for disrespect, and often led with force rather than
finesse. Yet, working with him helped me see just how complex people can
be. We all carry burdens that make life harder—not only for ourselves, but
also for the people who love us.

As Martin Luther King, Jr. said, "There is some good in the worst of us
and some evil in the best of us." Whatever was driving my father's actions
made him human—just like you and me. I've come to understand him more
now because I see my own complexity.

The pace was relentless, and the pay didn't match the effort required. I
wanted to keep my promise to him, but I also had to be honest with myself
and fair to my family. After six months, I decided to try to renegotiate for a
more balanced arrangement.

I told my father that although I had promised to help, I couldn't keep working nearly twenty-four hours a day at the current pay rate. I explained that I still
wanted to work for him if he would pay me for each hour I worked. I proposed
$1.75 an hour, the same rate as the workers I was supervising. His response, "No."

Though disappointed, I was learning that each experience was helping me
grow, and that if I trusted God, I could go further. I quit, parked his truck,
and walked five miles home.

PRESSURE FOR PURPOSE

Although working for my father was physically and mentally exhausting, I
am grateful to him for helping me develop a stronger work ethic and mental resilience. My time working for him revealed potential within me that I
didn't know existed.

While I say it was difficult to work for my father, the same has been said
about me. It's the fine line between demand and devotion, pressure and

purpose. Some call it grit; others call it guts. On the other side of my complaint was this: he didn't ask me to work for him, and I agreed to the pay rate. I was initially happy with the arrangement until I realized what it required.

As I mentioned in Chapter 1, Lesson 2, I ran away from home because I was expected to work tirelessly and give my earnings to him to support his family. Yet, when I needed a job, I returned to what was familiar without considering why I had left in the first place.

Maybe the reason I left matters less than the reason I returned. I didn't go back to work for my father because I was lost. I returned because there was still something I needed to receive from him.

My father gave me my first opportunity to lead. He trusted me with his business records, which taught me the skills necessary to run a business. During those long hours, he was my mentor, sharing lessons that have helped me and my family live a better life.

I have come to believe that people don't teach you; they give you the opportunity to learn from them. My father didn't just pass down a trade: he gave me space to discover more of who I am. That space gave me the confidence to envision something greater for myself and the audacity to pursue it. Watching him gave me permission to try, to fail, and to rise again.

But before that, something even deeper happened in the field: dirt beneath my boots, wind pressing against my chest, tears streaming down my face. I didn't just accept Christ—I surrendered. In that surrender, I found humility: the willingness to let go of the burdens I once clung to and the openness to embrace what I previously resisted.

Real spiritual growth is not a redo of the past; it is a sacred invitation to step into the future you are being shaped for—wiser, gentler, and finally ready to listen.

Some adult children avoid their parents not because they don't care, but because going back reopens old wounds. Some parents carry their own pain, unresolved and unspoken. Hurt does not live in just one generation; it passes through silence, misunderstanding, and survival.

Being a child does not automatically mean innocence—it often means you have not fully understood and taken responsibility for the impact of your choices. Likewise, being a parent does not make you right; everyone makes mistakes, and both parents and children need grace.

Had I stayed away from my father, I would have missed what God had waiting for me—not comfort or closure, but a skill, a challenge, and a vision for my future. That's the thing about returning: it is not always about being understood; it is about becoming someone who can understand. And that shift—your willingness to face the unknown—is often where God meets you.

WALKING INTO MYSELF

During my walk home, I reflected on many lessons, one of which was this: it is not just about the dollars you earn, but also what it takes to earn them. I also realized that while working alongside my father, a seed had been planted and it had taken root. If he could successfully run a business, then so could I.

My achievements, along with his affirmations of my ability, deepened my understanding of my potential. Have you ever had a moment when someone challenged you in a way that made you see yourself differently—more capable than you believed?

As my vision became clearer and a plan took shape, my excitement grew. My steps became steadier, and my pace quicker. I was eager to begin. I knew exactly what I had to accomplish immediately, in this order: buy a truck, get some tools, and secure a contract.

While this may sound like a sad ending, it isn't. I gave my father my best and he knew it. He felt my love and saw my commitment to him, and our relationship continued until his passing.

PAUSE + REFLECT

Sometimes God takes you back—not to punish or trap you—but to unlock something within you that can only be found in the places you tried to leave behind. Even roles that seem limiting can serve as lessons for the calling already inside you.

Before moving forward, ask: What is God teaching you through the people, patterns, and pushbacks you would rather avoid?

REFLECTION PROMPTS

- Is there a place or relationship God is inviting you to revisit—not for comfort, but for clarity?

_____

_____

_____

- What role has work played in shaping how you see your worth?

_____

_____

_____

- Are you missing a divine whisper because you're focusing on escaping a situation instead of growing through it?

_____

_____

_____

NO IS GOOD

THE SETUP IN THE SHUTDOWN

Your word is a lamp to guide my feet
and a light for my path.

PSALM 119:105

HOLDING ONTO THE DREAM

The next day, I woke up feeling refreshed, motivated by the idea of starting my own business and building a better future for my family.

I still hadn't shared my plan with Shirl. At the time, our firstborn was seven months old, and she was nearing the end of her fourth month of pregnancy with our second child. Those circumstances weighed heavily on my mind, but that wasn't the only reason I kept quiet.

I felt a strong sense of responsibility to figure things out on my own. I didn't want to burden my wife with uncertainty about how I would support our family. I believed it was my role to carry that weight.

In addition, expressing my thoughts and feelings had always been difficult, especially in the past. Sometimes I didn't know what to say; other times, I wasn't sure how to say it. As I stepped out the door that day, I finally shared my plan. Thankfully, Shirl believed in me and trusted my decisions, even when I didn't share every detail.

It was a bright, cool October morning when I started walking south. We owned a car, but I would not leave my family without transportation. After walking eight miles, I spotted a red Ford truck gleaming in the sunlight at a used car lot. From a distance, it looked perfect for what I had in mind.

As I walked onto the lot, a cheerful salesman, about five-foot-six-inch-tall, with bright red hair and a warm smile, greeted me. His friendly demeanor immediately put me at ease.

"Hi, I'm Russo," he said enthusiastically. "Do you see anything you like?"

"Yes, I like this truck," I replied. "I'm starting a business and need a reliable vehicle."

I kept talking, sharing my dream, hoping Russo would see where I was coming from and respond with compassion.

And he did. With each word I spoke, he smiled, his eyes lighting up as he nodded eagerly, ready for whatever I said next.

"I know how you feel," he said supportively. "I have just the thing for you. I'm here to help."

But there was a problem—one I hadn't mentioned. Maybe it was fear, shame, or just the thinking of a twenty-two-year-old chasing a dream he hadn't fully figured out. Whatever the reason, I never told him I didn't have any money.

As we were finalizing the deal, I finally confessed, "I don't have any money right now, but I'll postdate the check for the full amount one month from today."

Without hesitation, Russo said, "No problem."

We signed the agreement. I drove off the lot, filled the truck with gas, and headed home, excited to show Shirl and plan my next steps.

By early afternoon, Russo called.

"William, I need to deposit the check today," he said, his voice laced with urgency. "I need the money."

"No, you can't deposit that check," I said, confused and a bit frustrated. Slowing my voice, I added, "There isn't enough money in the account; it will bounce."

Silence hung in the air as I weighed my options. He had every right to cash the check, and the bank would likely honor it. The only option was to return the truck and get my check.

DEAL FALLS APART

I broke the silence. "I'll bring your truck back."

"Okay," he said with a hint of disappointment in his tone.

When I arrived, Russo met me outside. He inspected the truck, then handed me my check. I began my thirteen-mile walk north, fueled by a renewed sense of purpose.

True or not, I got the sense he never planned to wait the full thirty days. The nice-guy act had fooled me. Based on what I'd shared, I believe he thought I was desperate—and that a little pressure might push me into a situation where I'd find the money. But I knew my values, my limits, and what I was willing to do without risking my family.

HEADING NORTH

I knew exactly where I was going and what I needed to do next. I didn't know how things would unfold, but I had a feeling that I was headed in the right direction.

Psalm 119:105 says, "Your word is a lamp to guide my feet and a light for my path." At the time, I wasn't deeply familiar with God's Word, but I can say with certainty He was with me.

As I passed our trailer, I thought about my family inside. With each step, I rehearsed what I would say and reminded myself that giving up was not an option.

When I arrived at the Chevrolet dealership where I had purchased my first car, I walked in as if I had a million dollars in my pocket. A salesperson greeted me. I asked to speak with Mr. Roberts, the owner.

As he stepped out of his office and headed toward me, I began walking toward him. We stopped in front of each other, and I introduced myself.

"I don't have any money or credit," I said plainly. "I need a truck to start my business." Humbly, I continued, "I can write you a postdated check for the full amount, dated thirty days from now."

When I stopped talking, he studied me for a moment.

"I know you from somewhere," he said.

I remained silent.

"Did you work for Johnny Marino?"

"Yes," I answered, proud that he remembered me.

After a brief conversation, Mr. Roberts went back to his office. I watched as he made a phone call, likely confirming my identity, character, and work ethic.

When he returned, he said, "You know what?" I listened. "I'll let you have the truck. But instead of paying in one month, I'll give you a three-month payment plan."

DIVINE INTERVENTION

My heart raced, and my palms grew sweaty with disbelief. Twice in one day, I had been surprised. I wasn't judging the events—I was just trying to make sense of them. What was happening to me, and more importantly, what was God doing for me?

This time, He used Mr. Roberts to do more than I could have asked for or imagined.

Looking back, I'm reminded of Ephesians 3:20: "Now all glory to God, who is able, through his mighty power at work within us, to accomplish infinitely more than we might ask or think."

Later, I realized the Ford truck wasn't big enough to haul all the tools I needed for the job. God had protected me from making a short-sighted decision. Russo closed the wrong door, and Mr. Roberts opened the right one.

Through that, I learned a deeper truth about provision: it's not just about fulfilling a plan; it's also about preserving your purpose.

Through that encounter, God revealed a deeper truth I hadn't even recognized. Sometimes we judge the person who doesn't give us what we want and label them the enemy—when, in fact, God is using them just as intentionally as the one who is helping us. Divine redirection is just as important as direction.

Sometimes the most faithful thing we can do is walk away from a person, a position, or even an opportunity, so God can lead us into alignment with His will.

I was still new in my walk with God, but I was beginning to recognize His rhythm. He was guiding my steps by showing me how to learn instead of judge, stay open to the unexpected, and trust that He knows what I need, even when I think I know what I want.

CALLED—THEN TRUSTED

At the time, I didn't fully understand what had happened, but I knew God was at work. That's the thing about faith: you often see the results before you understand the plan.

As Isaiah 55:8–9 says, "'My thoughts are nothing like your thoughts,' says the LORD. 'And my ways are far beyond anything you could imagine. For just as the heavens are higher than the earth, so my ways are higher than your ways, and my thoughts higher than your thoughts.'"

But there's more. Romans 8:28 reminds us, "And we know that God causes everything to work together for the good of those who love God and are called according to his purpose for them." You might be wondering, *Am I called?* I believe we all are.

The real question is, "Have I answered the call?" That goes deeper than accepting Christ—it's about trusting Him and allowing Him to guide your steps. Answering the door is the first step. Once He enters your heart, you must decide what kind of relationship you want with Him.

I didn't have the words for it then, but I was beginning to understand that faith wasn't just believing—it was allowing yourself to be changed by that belief. Salvation and surrender had found me, but true conversion— real transformation—remained something I was still growing into, even now.

As I drove off the lot, I realized God was with me and within me. That realization gave me the courage to take the next step: finding a business that would sell me the tools I needed—on credit.

PAUSE + REFLECT

Not every "yes" is a blessing, and not every "no" is a loss. Sometimes, God interrupts your plans to protect you. What feels like rejection may actually be grace, guiding you toward what you didn't even realize you needed.

Discernment deepens when you ask mature questions—not "Can I?" but "Should I?" Not "Is it open?" but "Is this aligned with Your will for my life?" Often, the one thing you wanted to work—but didn't—is making room for something more aligned with your purpose.

REFLECTION PROMPTS

- Can you recall a time when something felt right at first but didn't go as planned? What was it, and what did you eventually learn was actually happening?

- How do you respond when a door is shut that you believed should have been opened?

- What could shift inside you and for you if you saw delay as divine guidance?

FAITH WITH BACKBONE

GOD AND GRIT

Choose a good reputation over great riches;
being held in high esteem is better than silver or gold.

PROVERBS 22:1

GOD AND GRIT

Driving off the lot felt miraculous. I believed God could do it, but when He did, it still took my breath away. Not because I doubted Him, but because I could see how deeply He had been involved all along.

God's hand wasn't just present; it was precise. His purpose and provision weren't just appearing in the moment: they had been at work behind the scenes the entire time.

As I drove down the highway toward HA Supplies and Tools, a company I hoped would provide the tools, I still didn't know if they'd be willing to help. But after experiencing the power of God's presence so clearly, I knew I had to try.

With only my reputation as currency, how else could a young Black man in 1961 find himself in this position?

When I arrived at HA Supplies and Tools, a family-owned business, I pushed aside every thought about money, race, and age. Instead, I focused on what God had already done.

I reminded myself that doubt makes you appear fearful and nervous. From experience, I knew fear shows up in my voice, body language, and eyes—making me seem suspicious even when I'm telling the truth.

If I showed up timid and they turned me down, I would have no one to blame but myself. It wouldn't be because I was young, Black, or lacked money; it would be because I lacked faith in God and confidence in myself. Doubt kills opportunity—convincing you to back away before you've even gotten started.

FAITH AND FAVOR

With purpose, I stepped inside, where a man, over six feet tall, wearing a stern expression, greeted me.

"Can I help you?" he asked.

Drawing on the confidence I had gained from the truck deal, I replied, "I hope so." I grounded myself, aiming to balance confidence with humility. "I'm starting a business and need some tools."

"Okay," he said, encouraging me to continue.

I took a deep breath.

"Hi, I'm William. Before we go any further, I need to tell you that I don't have any money," I said plainly.

He looked at me intensely, his expression sharpening.

His tone carried a trace of irritation and sarcasm. He frowned and asked, "How do you expect to get tools if you don't have any money?"

Holding his gaze, I answered, "I hope you'll trust me."

"Trust you?" he snapped, disbelief clear in his voice. "Trust you how?"

I paused to steady myself.

"If you trust me, I'll pay you everything I owe—one month from today," I said, my voice calm and firm.

He studied me, his expression shifting between contempt and curiosity.

"You've got a lot of nerve," he said. "I've never seen you before, and you walk in here off the street expecting me to take your word." He paused. "You could take my tools and never come back."

I nodded and met his gaze. "Yes, I could. But I won't. I'll do exactly what I said. And if something happens and I can't pay, I promise I'll come back and we'll talk about other arrangements."

He stared at me in silence, maybe for five minutes, wrestling with the question: Can I trust him? I said nothing, letting him decide.

At last, his expression softened. "So, what tools do you need?"

Relieved, I said, "A wheelbarrow, a flat shovel, a round-point shovel, a concrete rake, a trowel, and a metal float."

As I spoke, he began writing.

With a firm but measured tone, he called over an employee and handed him the list. "Go upstairs and get these items."

When the tools were brought down, he asked, "Are these what you need?"

"Yes."

He looked me in the eye. "I'm going to trust you, and I expect you to keep your word."

"I will," I said sincerely. "Thank you. I won't disappoint you."

He told me he was the owner and instructed me to pay him directly.

As I started wheeling the tools toward the door, he called out, "Wait a minute. I'm Joel."

He then bent down, picked up a wooden float, and handed it to me.

"You might have some use for this, William."

I met his gaze. "Thank you, Joel," I repeated as the weight of the moment settled in.

Pushing open the door, I walked to my truck, my heart full.

I didn't just leave with tools—I left with a deeper understanding of what it means to walk by faith. Even without knowing all the answers, I understood this: God was showing me why I should trust Him. And even now, I continue to be in awe of how He moved that day.

PAUSE + REFLECT

Faith isn't just belief; it's boldness. It's the courage to move forward when there's no money, no clear plan, and all you have to offer is your name and your word. That's when faith grows legs and character shows its true value.

REFLECTION PROMPTS

- When was the last time you had to trust God and stand firm, not because you were confident about the outcome, but because you knew who He is?

_____

_____

_____

- When have you had to rely on your reputation as your "currency"? What did that moment reveal about your integrity, your faith, and your follow-through?

_____

_____

_____

- When no one else can vouch for you except God, how do you carry yourself in spirit, posture, and speech?

_____

_____

_____

CHAPTER 4

GROWING INTO THE PROMISE

TRUST: A SACRED ASSIGNMENT

*Trust in the Lord with all your heart and lean not
on your own understanding; in all your ways submit
to him, and he will make your paths straight.*

PROVERBS 3:5–6

S. RENEE'S MOMENTS TO MEASURE

CHAPTER 4

Whether you stand firm or stumble forward, God is already there, responding to your whisper or guiding you through challenges that test your beliefs. What starts as fear can become faith if you're willing to trust what He's building in you.

Growing Into the Promise encourages you to recognize how God works through small affirmations, divine provisions, and the weight of responsibility—stretching your capacity to trust Him.

In Lessons 10–12, you'll understand:

- How powerfully God can move in your life when you fully surrender.

- Miracles don't just open doors; they also stretch your belief.

- Favor reflects God's trust in you; your response reveals your trust in Him.

- Provision isn't just help; it's an invitation to grow into what you've prayed for.

ANSWERED IN THE NIGHT

CLARITY IN THE MORNING

For God speaks again and again, though people do not recognize it.
He speaks in dreams, in visions of the night, when
deep sleep falls on people as they lie in their beds.

JOB 33:14-15

GOD, SHOW ME

The next day, I woke up early. Shirl made breakfast and packed my lunch, just as she always did. By 6 a.m., I was on the road driving thirty-five miles north to an area where new housing projects were underway.

The sun shone through the windshield, warming my face and lifting my spirits. But beneath the calm, one question lingered: What if I don't get hired?

My ability to keep the promises I had made to everyone who believed in me, Shirl, Mr. Roberts, and Joel, depended entirely on securing a contract. That pressure weighed heavily on me.

I believed it was possible to get work, but I wasn't sure if it would happen, especially within the tight timeframe I was working within. I swung between faith and fear, doubt and confidence. But even with uncertainty, I pushed through my discomfort. I had to see what God had planned for me, trusting that everything He had already done had purpose.

I arrived at the construction company's office around 6:45 a.m. It wasn't opened yet, so I stayed in the truck and watched. Around 7:30, I saw some movement and figured they had come in through the back door.

I took a deep breath, stepped out of the truck, opened the front door, and walked inside. A man I assumed was the owner, along with the superintendent, approached.

The owner greeted me, but before he could say more, the superintendent stepped forward and asked, "What can I do for you?"

I inhaled, rolled my shoulders back, and lifted my head. "I'm looking for work," I said.

The owner began walking away as the superintendent asked, "What can you do?"

"I can pour concrete," I answered.

As I spoke, the owner paused and turned slightly, as if he wanted to hear what I was going to say next. My doubts resurfaced—I was sure he was thinking I was too young.

I added quickly, "I can also build steps and lay sidewalks," trying to sound more seasoned.

The owner turned completely around, walked over, and said, "Richard, you know, we could use a man like this. We're short on help."

The superintendent asked, "Okay, what else do you know?"

Before I could answer, he walked behind the desk and pulled out a blueprint—a technical drawing outlining how a structure should be built.

He handed it to me and said, "Come back tomorrow with a price for the concrete work."

I assumed his impatience stemmed from how young I looked, or maybe he didn't appreciate his boss stepping in and telling him to take me seriously. Whatever the reason, I smiled, confidently took the blueprint, and replied, "Sure."

I climbed into my truck and drove straight home. Not once, from the moment I took the blueprint until I opened it, did it occur to me that I had never seen one before.

GIVING UP

When I got home and settled in, I sat at the kitchen table and unrolled the blueprint. I couldn't believe my eyes—lines, numbers, boxes, and material specifications were everywhere. I had no idea what I was looking at or where to begin.

I sat for hours, staring at it, studying it, trying to make sense of the unfamiliar markings. The longer I looked, the more overwhelmed I felt. Doubt crept in like a slow fog. I wondered, Was I in over my head?

I wanted to believe I had come this close for a reason, but I couldn't see it. I was discouraged, and unsure of what to do next. None of it made sense. Not only could I not read the blueprint, but I was on the edge of success and couldn't reach it.

As night fell and the sky darkened, I finally gave up. I stopped fighting and let go.

"There's nothing I can do with this," I told Shirl.

I carefully folded the blueprint and paused, thinking maybe I missed something, anything. When I had exhausted everything I knew, I put it in my truck.

I was deflated, wondering how something that felt so right could go so wrong. Morning was approaching, and I still had no numbers—no breakdown of hours, no material costs—to justify my time or land the contract. What was going on? I knew I had the skills; I just didn't know how to calculate the costs. Within twenty-four hours, I'd gone from the mountaintop to the valley. I accepted that it was over and went to bed with the blueprint, and my problems, on my mind.

CLARITY COMES

Around 3 a.m., a sudden vision of the blueprint jolted me awake. I jumped out of bed, grabbed my pants, and hurriedly pulled them on—startling Shirl from her sleep.

Groggy and curious, she asked, "What are you doing?"

It felt like something had been unlocked in my mind, like a switch had flipped.

"That print," I said, eyes wide, "I can read it!"

Confused, "What?" Shirl asked.

"I can read the blueprint," I repeated, still in disbelief.

I ran outside, grabbed the blueprint from the truck, and unrolled it. Everything on that oversized paper made perfect sense. It was clear—as if I'd been reading blueprints my entire life. I calculated the cost for the job, and Shirl drafted the estimate.

I still can't fully explain what happened; all I know is that it did. From that day forward, I could read blueprints and calculate costs for government, state, commercial, and residential buildings.

But this miraculous moment also taught me a few other things: Surrender and silence were part of the answer. It wasn't the solution I had earned, but the reassurance I needed. And surrender can look like giving up or giving in. It's when you're at your weakest, most vulnerable moment that God shows up and reminds you, He's been with you all along.

One of our greatest frustrations tends to come from wanting to know what God knows—sometimes so much so that we never fully surrender. We often focus more on knowing than on trusting.

God communicates with everyone differently and at different times. In this case, it was at the third hour of a new day when He appeared, not with noise but with clarity. And although it was technically morning, it was at my darkest hour, right in the middle of the night.

This I know for sure: God had rescued me not only from losing the opportunity but also from the embarrassment of returning to the office empty-handed. I wasn't just prepared for the meeting—I wasn't going alone. By 5 a.m., I was on the road, heading north to submit my first bid.

PAUSE + REFLECT

Sometimes, your mind becomes quiet not because you're at peace, but because you've run out of options. When you stop struggling, you open the door for divine grace to step in and elevate what you, on your own, could never achieve.

REFLECTION PROMPTS

- What challenge are you still trying to solve with God?

  _____

  _____

  _____

- What can happen if you stop trying to control the outcome?

  _____

  _____

  _____

- How might your actions change if you do your part and trust that God has done His?

  _____

  _____

  _____

FAITHFUL HEART, FEARFUL MIND

WRESTLING TO WIN

And I am certain that God, who began the good work
within you, will continue his work until it is finally
finished on the day when Christ Jesus returns.

PHILIPPIANS 1:6

WAITING TESTS FAITH

I arrived early and parked in front of the office, just as I had the day before. As I waited for the doors to open, I sat in stillness, replaying the last two days as I prepared myself for whatever might come next.

If I secured this contract, then in three days I would have exactly what I had prayed for: a truck, some tools, and a job. It was the kind of favor I had been reading about in the Bible, and now it was unfolding in my own life. There was no other explanation—God was clearly at work.

Still, I found myself asking, "What if the superintendent says no?" Even as I stood in the evidence of His grace and power, I wrestled with doubt. It wasn't whether He could do it, but whether He would—and whether I was even worthy to receive such a great gift. It was a strange, very human dilemma.

When the lights came on, I stepped inside with the blueprint and proposal in hand. Approaching the superintendent, I hesitated—unsure if he recognized me or was simply surprised to see me.

I started to reintroduce myself, but he cut me off: "Yes, I remember you. What do you have for me?"

I handed him my proposal. As he read, I kept my gaze low, trying to catch a clue in his expression—would it be yes or no?

"Are you sure you can do this work?" he finally asked.

Caught off guard, I paused, choosing my words carefully. "Yes, I'm sure I can do it, if you can hire me," I replied.

He leaned forward. "That's not the problem. We furnish the concrete and all the materials. It's an investment. What if you mess it up? What then?"

Feeling the opportunity slipping away, I said, "If you're not satisfied, you don't owe me a dime."

He looked up. "Are you sure?"

"Yes, I'm sure."

He paused, then asked, "When do you want to start?"

"Now, if it's alright with you."

"Then let's get to it," he said eagerly.

He led me to his vehicle and motioned for me to get in. As we drove through the development, he pointed out the houses he wanted me to work on. On the way back, he explained the pay schedule: bills need to be in the 15th of each month, and checks are available for pickup on the 20th.

As a new business owner, I was thrilled to land my first contract, not by connections or credentials, but by faith, favor, and a willingness to show up.

I started working right away but quickly realized I needed help. Before heading home that evening, I drove to the street where men hung out, hoping someone would hire them. I met a man named Charlie and told him what I needed.

"I'll be here waiting for you in the morning," he said.

LET THE WORK BE THE WITNESS

Each day, Charlie and I worked from sunrise to sunset, completing everything on time. On the 15th, I dropped Charlie off at the jobsite to start working, and I drove to the office. I sat in my truck until Richard pulled up. We walked inside together.

The owner was there when we arrived. We greeted him. "Good morning."

Richard turned to me and asked, "What do you have?"

I handed him my bill, sealed in an envelope.

He opened it, glanced at the numbers, and asked, "You got all this done?"

"Yes, sir. Every bit of it," I replied proudly.

"Completed?" he pressed.

"Yes, sir." I nodded.

The owner chimed in, "The only way to be sure is to let him show you what he has done."

We got into his car and drove to the worksite. House by house, we walked the job, and Richard didn't say a word. Though I was confident in our work, the silence made me uneasy. I wanted to ask what he thought, but I didn't. And he didn't offer.

The ride back to the office was just as quiet. As soon as we stepped inside, the owner asked, "What did you find out?"

"I'll tell you one thing, that's some of the best work we've had done around here," Richard answered.

I stood quietly, holding my breath as he continued.

"Everything is clean, backfilled, and done neatly."

The owner, amazed, asked, "All of it?"

"Yes," Richard replied.

"Well, he must have had a lot of help," the owner responded.

I smiled to myself, knowing it had been just Charlie and me putting in those long, exhausting hours. But I also knew it wasn't only us. God had honored our efforts—and His favor spoke louder than anything I could say or do on my own.

As I turned to leave and get back to work, Richard reminded me, "Your check will be available on the 20th at 3 p.m."

LEARNING TO HOLD IT

I still found it hard to believe that God had blessed me in this way. I felt a constant tension between His unfolding provision and my ability to recognize and accept the depth of His love.

For five days, I wondered if I would get paid. My mind churned with conflicting thoughts about how this would turn out. *Was this a trick? Had I been scammed?*

Even though I prayed and reminded myself that God was in control, the questions kept coming. I wanted to trust what was happening, but I didn't yet know how to live in that trust.

Then, on the 20th at 3 p.m., I went to the office—and my check was waiting for me.

I walked back to my truck, sat down, and just stared at it, overwhelmed with gratitude. I had earned more in a single month than I had in the past six months combined. Holding that check felt like proof that my work had value. Yet somehow, it still didn't feel real.

Is this check even cashable? Will it bounce?

I needed to be sure. I drove back to the jobsite and told Charlie, "Load up. We'll come back tomorrow." I believed, yet part of me still expected something to go wrong.

Fifteen minutes later, I walked into a bank that cashed checks for non–account holders. As I stepped inside, another wave of doubt hit: *Will they really give me the money?*

They did—no delays, no questions. I left clutching the bag, half convinced someone might try to snatch it. Back in the truck, I paid Charlie and slid the bag under the seat. After dropping him off, I drove straight home, still trapped in my own anxious loop: *Would someone take this from me? Did God really do this for me?*

I was young, scared, and fragile—still learning how to live in the reality of an answered prayer. I didn't know how to manage my mind or emotions.

Everything in my life was shifting: my relationship with God, my family, my client, even Charlie. But the biggest change was happening inside me. I was beginning to see myself differently. I wasn't just a worker or a provider anymore; I was someone God trusted with greater responsibility.

That realization was both a blessing and a challenge. It takes maturity to receive what you've asked for, and growth to carry it. You've probably heard the saying, "Watch what you pray for." It's often used casually, but it deserves to be taken seriously.

You ask, and God will answer. The deeper question is: Are you ready to receive it?

FINALLY FREE

When I got home, I felt safe. For the first time in days, I could breathe freely. It felt good to celebrate with Shirl; we had never seen so much money in our lives.

We emptied the bag onto the table, spread the bills out, and stared in disbelief. Then, like two kids in pure joy, we tossed the money into the air—thanking God, laughing, and soaking in the moment.

That celebration wasn't just about provision—it was about freedom. It reminded me that God's blessings aren't only about what we receive; they're an invitation to grow, to trust, and to become the people He's calling us to be. In this case, He called us together.

In that moment, we were two joyful people, overwhelmed by the abundance of His goodness. The next day, every dollar was deposited in the bank—but something deeper had been planted in us: a faith strong enough to believe in possibility.

PAUSE + REFLECT

Sometimes it's not the miracle you doubt—it's yourself. When God moves on your behalf, fear and insecurity can cloud your vision. You question your readiness, your worthiness, and whether it's all too good to be true.

But grace doesn't require your perfection, only your participation. As God provides, He also prepares you: stretching your faith, reshaping your mindset, and enlarging your capacity to carry what He's entrusted to you with wisdom and maturity.

REFLECTION PROMPTS

- Have you ever wondered if you were prepared for what you prayed for?

_____

_____

_____

- How has fear attempted to rewrite the story God is creating in your life?

_____

_____

_____

- How is your relationship with yourself evolving as you learn to accept God's provision?

  _____

  _____

  _____

FAITH ON CREDIT

CAN GOD TRUST YOU?

*Abraham never wavered in believing God's promise. In fact, his
faith grew stronger, and in this he brought glory to God. He was
fully convinced that God is able to do whatever he promises.*

ROMANS 4:20-21

BUILDING TRUST

Within thirty days, I returned to the Chevrolet dealership to pay off the truck, then headed to HA Supplies and Tools to settle the debt for the tools. As I walked in, Joel's curious gaze made it clear he hadn't expected me to come back.

But I did—not just to pay the bill, but to keep my word.

He looked down at me; I looked up at him. Smiling, I handed him the full payment. At first, his face was unreadable, but then something in him softened.

"I trusted you with my tools," he said, "and in good faith, you've paid for them. For whatever you need, you have credit here."

Then, with gentle warmth, he continued, "We have a lumber yard up the street. It's on the corner. You've got credit there, too. If anyone questions you, tell them Joel sent you." I thanked him and, holding back my emotions, walked out of the store.

That moment deepened my trust in God, renewed my faith in people's goodness, and reminded me of the person I was becoming.

When I started my business, all I knew was that I needed a truck, some tools, and a job. I didn't know if I could pay Joel or Mr. Roberts, but I intended to. Looking back, I can see that God knew my heart and helped me honor that intention. As 1 Chronicles 28:9 reminds us, "For the Lord sees every heart and knows every plan and thought. If you seek him, you will find him."

He was teaching me to trust Him and showing me that He opens doors no one else can. I didn't know what my future held, but I was ready to act. That season taught me a lasting truth: we don't need to spend our lives trying to prove ourselves to God. He already knows who we are—even better, He wants to reveal Himself to us.

Paul wrote in 1 Corinthians 2:9, "No eye has seen, no ear has heard, and no mind has imagined what God has prepared for those who love him."

It was God who moved on the hearts of Mr. Roberts and Joel to recognize my sincerity. And what about the construction company owner who unexpectedly stepped in, urging the superintendent to consider me? What were the chances of him standing there at that exact moment?

None of these were random events. They were moments only God could orchestrate.

And think about this: These were company owners. While every person in an organization matters, I didn't have to fight through layers of approval or navigate human barriers—I had direct access to the decision-makers.

God gave me that access.

He was trusting me with people, opportunities, and provision. I was being positioned—but none of it came without responsibility. I had to steward everything He placed in my hands with integrity and gratitude.

For moments like this, I reflect on Matthew 25:23: "Well done, my good and faithful servant. You have been faithful in handling this small amount, so now I will give you many more responsibilities. Let's celebrate together!"

While that verse often points to eternity, I've come to believe it also speaks to our lives now. God honors faithfulness—in the small things, in quiet moments we might overlook, and in the daily commitments we choose to uphold.

BELIEVING IN POSSIBILITY

As shared in Chapter 3, Lesson 7, when I parked my father's truck and began the long walk home, I was inspired and committed to start my own business.

I moved forward in faith—even when my stomach was tied in knots—and God met me in motion at every turn. Jesus says in Matthew 17:20, "I tell you the truth, if you had faith even as small as a mustard seed, you could say to this mountain, 'Move from here to there,' and it would move. Nothing would be impossible."

When strangers went beyond their standard protocols to help me, I saw this scripture come to life. And when it did, I realized something important: It's not just about the mountain being moved—it's about what you choose to do once it's no longer there.

That's when I began to understand: integrity isn't only about whether you can keep your word, but whether you will.

Listening and acting on what you hear activates the favor already present in your life. Whether you're standing firm in confidence or trembling as you try to trust Him, your faith—however small—is enough to see and experience God's presence and power at work.

BUILDING BY FAITH

In just a few years, God poured blessings on Shirl and me faster than we could've imagined or fully comprehended. By the time Shirl was twenty and I was twenty-four, we had three children, had purchased land, upgraded to a larger trailer, and bought a brand-new 1963 Chevrolet Impala.

A few years later, when Shirl turned twenty-four and I was twenty-seven, we had four children—two boys and two girls—which meant we needed more space. So, we decided it was time to build our first home. But when we applied for financing, the bank rejected our application. Their response was, "Build the house first, and then we'll give you a mortgage." In other words, they expected a finished house before lending us a dime.

We had money in the bank, assets, and a thriving business, so their refusal didn't make sense then—and still doesn't today.

Ordinarily, that kind of rejection might have discouraged us. But by then, our faith had grown strong. We were in church every Sunday unless someone was sick, and we were deeply involved. More than just attendance, our lives were grounded in the Word.

So instead of seeing a dead end, we turned to Scripture. One verse that gave us courage was 1 Corinthians 1:27: "Instead, God chose things the world considers foolish in order to shame those who think they are wise. And he chose things that are powerless to shame those who are powerful."

That verse reminded us that roadblocks, barriers, and dead ends mean nothing to those who believe. Even when logic fails, we can trust that God is working behind the scenes in ways we can't yet see. The hardest part is being patient—waiting to see how His plan unfolds. So, with some creative thinking, I began searching for another path forward.

I went back to HA Supplies and Tools, this time speaking with Joel's brother and sister, who co-owned the business. I told them about our growing family and our dream to build a home.

I explained, "The bank has promised to mortgage the house if I finish it within seven months. What I need from you is the material to build it."

They listened carefully, then asked, "Have you ever built a house before?"

"No," I said. "But I'm going to build this one."

They exchanged glances, raising their eyebrows.

I laid out what I needed: all the supplies to build a 1,500-square-foot house with a full basement. There was one snag—I wanted the house built entirely of brick, and they didn't sell bricks. Even that wasn't a dealbreaker. They agreed to purchase the brick from a supplier.

In the end, they financed the entire project.

After coming home from work each day, Shirl and I went straight to the plot where our future home would stand. We worked six days a week, driven by faith and focused on the vision we believed God had placed in our hearts.

S. Renee was just three months old, but our three oldest children worked alongside us. My philosophy was simple: if you can walk, you can work.

As we stayed focused on the task at hand, the noise around us grew louder. People were talking—not to us, but about us. Whispers from friends, church members, and even family eventually made their way back to us.

I chose not to defend Shirl or myself. Trying to explain would have meant justifying what God was doing in our lives—and He didn't need defending. His glory shows when the time is right.

I'd smile and recall the saying, "If a dog brings a bone, he'll carry one." In other words, the same people repeating what others said were likely part of the conversation themselves. I learned that few will stand with you when the rest of the room is against you.

The message we kept hearing was clear: they'll never finish that house. But with every nail driven and every brick laid, the vision came to life. What others doubted, criticized, and dismissed rose before their eyes—and ours—one wall, one room, one act of faith at a time.

Our focus never shifted to proving people wrong. That kind of distraction would have derailed us. Instead, we tuned out the noise and stayed centered on the blessings God had for us. That focus helped us work faster and with fewer mistakes.

In seven months, the house we designed was completed. As promised, I went to the bank to secure the loan. It was approved, and I returned to HA Supplies and Tools to pay every dollar I owed—on time.

That house became more than just a home. It stood as a monument of faith, favor, and follow-through. But the true legacy wasn't the structure we built with our hands—it was the trust, endurance, and love God had been building in our hearts.

PAUSE + REFLECT

Trust is a sacred agreement.

Some blessings come with a silent question: Can God trust you to handle what you asked for with grace and gratitude? Whether it's a relationship or a resource, good stewardship shows maturity and growth.

Stewardship is less about proving yourself and more about aligning your actions with the trust God has already given: showing up with integrity, returning what you've borrowed, nurturing those entrusted to you, and remaining faithful. God invites you to actively engage in all that He has provided for you.

REFLECTION PROMPTS

- How do others' perceptions of you influence your decision-making?

_____

_____

_____

- What has God entrusted to you that you need to manage more faithfully?

_____

_____

_____

- In your work, relationships, or opportunities, where is God prompting you to grow in faithfulness?

_____

_____

_____

CHAPTER 5

THE BREAKING THAT BUILDS

BREAKING IS THE BRIDGE TO BECOMING

So after you have suffered a little while,
he will restore, support, and strengthen you,
and he will place you on a firm foundation.

1 PETER 5:10

S. RENEE'S MOMENTS TO MEASURE

CHAPTER 5

Some losses shake you, while others shape you. Chapter 5 covers both. It shows what happens when everything you've worked for suddenly falls apart and the world tries to make you believe you're not worthy, not wanted, and not enough.

But God doesn't just meet you in the fallout; He walks with you through it, shaping something within you. No matter what you've lost or who has tried to hold you back, it's not over.

God's plan is still unfolding, and it might begin right here in *The Breaking That Builds*, where you'll discover what it means to have your life rebuilt with His guidance.

In Lessons 13–15, you'll discover:

- You can navigate through complex and chaotic seasons of your life.

- Every step, situation, and circumstance holds meaning and contributes to your growth.

- When you feel lost or off course, God is guiding you to something special.

- It's not over; when God leads, the unexpected follows.

WHEN THE GATE LOCKS

LOSS THAT LEADS TO LIFE

My thoughts are nothing like your thoughts, says the Lord.
And my ways are far beyond anything you could imagine.
For just as the heavens are higher than the earth,
so my ways are higher than your ways and my thoughts
higher than your thoughts.

ISAIAH 55:8-9

THE RISE

Shirl and I were united—worshiping and working together as true partners in life, faith, and business. Every aspect of our lives was thriving. While she stayed home with our children, she also served as the business's secretary, managing the finances with the precision of a seasoned accountant.

I focused on generating income to ensure our family had food, shelter, clothing, medical care: everything we needed or wanted. Her unwavering support and sharp business sense propelled both my dreams and our lives forward.

Together, we were moving fast—building, growing, and adjusting to a new rhythm of life. In that momentum, I missed the warning signs. Without realizing it, I had begun trusting the pace more than the process. As soon as one project ended, another began. I stayed busy, and everything seemed to be running smoothly—until I slipped up.

I didn't follow through the way I normally would, and I got burned.

THE FALL

It was around 1968 or 1969, about a year after we moved into our new home. My company had secured a contract with a business that, on the surface, appeared financially sound. The owner projected what I called the "Big Man" image—driving a Cadillac, using a car phone (a rare luxury at the time), and carrying himself with a confidence that commanded attention.

The image was so convincing, I never thought to question whether the company was as solid as his image made it appear.

My team and I showed up like we did every day, early and ready to work. At first, nothing seemed unusual, but soon I noticed the other contractors packing up and leaving.

One of them looked over and asked, "What are you doing?"

"I'm working!" I replied, confused but focused on the job.

He shook his head and yelled over the noise, "Don't you know the company's bankrupt?"

"What?" I said, not fully understanding what he meant.

"The cops are about to lock the gate. No one's getting in or out."

I had never even heard the word *bankrupt*, so I kept working. But a few minutes later, something told me to walk up to the gate and see what was going on. When I got there, a police officer stood guard, already securing it with a padlock. Behind him, contractors had gathered in small groups, murmuring among themselves.

I asked, "What's going on?"

"We've locked this gate to prevent anyone from entering or exiting. This facility is being secured," he said.

"Secured?" I asked, startled.

"Yes, secured," he repeated firmly.

"I haven't heard anything about this. I have men inside working," I told him.

"Go get them—quick. I'll wait here until you return so I can let you out."

I rushed back to gather my crew, and as I did, I wondered about what this meant for the money he owed me—and the money I owed others. We had worked for months without payment issues, so when things got busy, I forgot to give Shirl the information she needed to submit the last two months of invoices—over $60,000. Life was good. Why worry?

Without explanation, I told the crew to pack up. We were leaving.

Once we got to the gate, the officer was still there, and the other contractors and crews were all waiting for the owner to arrive. But he never came. Eventually, we had no choice but to leave without answers.

I stayed calm as I spoke to my team of eight. I told them I didn't know what had happened or whether there would be more work, but I promised to keep them updated. Most importantly, I assured them they would be paid every dime they were owed.

THE SEARCH FOR ANSWERS

As I drove back to Dover, I couldn't believe what had just happened—but I didn't understand it well enough to know if I should be worried. Caught off guard by what people were saying, I was in shock, searching for answers. I kept wondering: *What did this mean? Had I become too comfortable relying on my perceptions instead of my prayers? Had that shift cost me—and Shirl—the business? What had I done?*

Eager for clarity, I wanted to hear Shirl's take. When I told her what had happened, she didn't believe it. I had always described how wealthy the man was, so the news didn't make sense—not to her, and not to me.

Still confused and searching for answers, I drove forty-five minutes back to the jobsite. The police officer was still there, standing guard at the locked gate. No one was allowed past the entrance to the office. Hoping for clarity, I went to see the supplier who had extended me credit for the concrete.

The moment I stepped inside, I sensed something was off. The usual clatter of forklifts and chatter of workers on radios had been replaced by quiet voices and sideways glances. I approached the owner and began to explain the situation. His expression—a mix of contempt and frustration—said more than his words ever could.

"We know all about that one," he said flatly. "We got hung up for quite a few dollars from that place. We don't know what's going to happen."

That's when it finally hit me: this was real. I wandered through the store aimlessly, trying to gather my thoughts and decide what to do next.

Eventually, I looked up, took a breath, and said, "Listen, I don't know how this is going to turn out, but I've got all my money tied up in this job." I paused, trying to find the right words. "I know I still owe you for the concrete, and I was planning to pay you as soon as the check came in."

He didn't say anything.

I took another breath. "I promise I'll pay what I owe you."

He listened, then shrugged his shoulders and, without expression or any sign that he believed me, simply said, "Okay."

Everything about his tone and body language suggested he wanted to say, "Whatever." And I got it. We had all been deceived. He didn't give me the answers I was hoping for, but his reaction told me enough—this situation was worse than I thought.

As I drove home, armed with a little more information but not enough to make a decision, I tried to figure out what to do next. The more I thought about it, the more my head hurt. I couldn't understand what had happened, let alone process it or come up with a solution.

HOLLOW DAYS

For three days, I didn't leave the house. I was in shock—feeling empty, lost, and vulnerable.

It felt as if someone had robbed me—and in a way, they had, legally. This situation didn't just hurt me; it impacted my entire family, and I worried it might damage my reputation with creditors.

Still, I clung to the hope that God would somehow work everything out. He always had before. And in the end, He did—though not in the way I expected. I kept praying. I kept hoping. I'm still not sure whether that was unwavering faith or just foolish thinking, but I believed I might recover at least a portion of what was owed—enough to keep the business alive.

That hope quickly faded when I learned that in bankruptcies, banks and the government have first claim. After they're paid, whatever remains is divided among others. In my case, nothing was left for contractors.

When I heard the news, I began to question my understanding of God's Word. And when I couldn't get an answer from Him, I turned inward and started asking myself:

> *Had I been so focused on success that I missed the warning signs?*
> *Did my drive to work hard cause me to overlook the business itself?*
> *If I had submitted my bill on time, would I have been paid or*
>   *at least seen a red flag?*
> *What could I have done differently to protect my family?*

Today, I don't believe anything I could have done would have changed the outcome. At that point in my journey, I had a lesson to learn. The only explanation that makes sense is this: God knew I needed that experience to reshape my thinking. Without it, I believe the cost of my unpreparedness might have been far greater.

I've come to understand that true success isn't measured by what you own but by who you are. You don't need to prove anything; you just need to show up as yourself.

For me, the greatest gift would not come from recovering what I had lost, but from what I didn't know was ahead. Back then, I thought the answer I needed was a check, a contract, or a second chance. But what God was building in me went deeper than anything money could restore. I was beginning to learn: sometimes the real breakthrough isn't around you—it's within you.

It began with learning to pause and pray, to make sure I was still walking with God. Even in that dark hour, I discovered, I was still on the right path.

LOOKING BACK

Now, with over fifty years of life and business experience behind me, I believe something deeper was at work—something I couldn't have possibly understood at the time.

Remember in Chapter 4, Lesson 11, when I shared my fear that someone would take my money? Back then, the worry felt foolish. But now I wonder: Did that fear really begin with the bag of money, or did it start much earlier—long before I ever held a paycheck in my hands?

When I was about nine years old, living in a labor camp, some of the adult workers would give me pennies, nickels, and dimes. To keep my savings safe, I used an old can about three inches tall, cutting a slit in the top to make a homemade piggy bank. For nearly a month, I saved every coin I received.

Each time I dropped a coin in, I'd shake the can just to hear the rattle— the sound reminding me it was getting fuller, and that soon I'd open it to see how much I had saved.

Every night, I'd climb into the top bunk and tuck the can under my arm as I slept. When I went out to work in the fields, I carefully hid it beneath the blankets. But one day, after work, I eagerly returned to my bed, like always, pulled back the covers—and my can was gone.

Someone had stolen my money.

I broke down crying.

The women gathered around to comfort me. "Don't worry about it," they said. "That's a terrible thing to do to a child." My brother was laughing. I felt ashamed. I kept wondering: Why did I hide it there? Why did I use a can? I blamed myself.

Word spread quickly, and after that, people gave me less. Maybe they thought I couldn't keep it safe, or maybe they sensed I couldn't handle the emotional weight if it happened again. It wasn't much, but I kept whatever I received in my pocket.

Looking back, I wonder: Did the decision made by that nine-year-old boy—who learned he couldn't trust himself or anyone else—influence how I felt and shape what I did decades later? Did that moment of lost trust contribute, in some way, to the downfall of my business? Was it a premonition of what was to come?

Or would it become a lesson in redemption—one God knew I would need to experience so I could learn to trust again?

I may never fully understand why it happened, but I believe it was necessary. God was preparing me for everything He already knew He would one day place in my hands.

PAUSE + REFLECT

Loss doesn't always mean failure; sometimes it's God's way of closing a gate you were never meant to enter—or stay in. What feels like punishment may actually be protection, a barrier meant to guide you toward a path that demands greater wisdom, deeper faith, and better stewardship.

There is a difference between being blessed and being ready to receive, steward, and live in the blessing. Over time, you shift from chasing blessings to embracing the lessons that help you recognize and appreciate the ones you have already received.

REFLECTION PROMPTS

- Have you ever experienced a loss that felt like failure, only to discover it was God's protection? What did it teach you?

- In which areas have you veered away from God's guidance? What is it costing you?

- What would you do differently if you trusted God not just for the blessing but for the strength and wisdom to sustain it?

LEANING IN

FAITH IN THE FACE OF INJUSTICE

Commit everything you do to the Lord.
Trust him, and he will help you.
He will make your innocence radiate like the dawn,
and the justice of your cause will shine like the noonday sun.

PSALM 37:5–6

THE WEIGHT OF STILLNESS

Over the next three days, as I struggled to accept my new reality, a deep emptiness settled in. The world kept moving, but I felt frozen in place. The first line in Psalm 46:10 says, "Be still, and know that I am God." But the truth was, I didn't know God well enough to be still. All I knew was how to take action and see God in the results.

But I couldn't see what action to take. No vision for my future. No dreams pointing me forward. No instincts whispering what to do next.

Stillness felt like silence—and it was suffocating. I felt like I was drowning—anxious, unsure of what had happened, why it had happened, or what I should do about it. I searched my heart for a "Word" and my thoughts for clarity, but found only chaos.

At twenty-nine, I had already faced challenges, but this one felt different. It wasn't just a setback—it felt like the ground beneath me was giving way. My beliefs about God, myself, and my future—all of it came under fire.

It's the kind of disorientation that follows major loss. You're left trying to figure out how to live in a reality you didn't choose. Your mind loops through the same questions over and over, never finding answers.

I couldn't shake the voices of those who said I'd never build the house, let alone run a business. Their words echoed louder as the truth of my situation sank in. I tried to think of ways to save the business, but none seemed viable. Every dollar had gone to payroll and bills, leaving almost nothing for our family. The skies were still clear, but a storm was closing in.

From where I stood, it looked like everything we'd worked for had been ripped away—suddenly and without warning. But as each day passed, I began to see something else: if I didn't act, my family wouldn't eat. In the stillness of that realization, a quiet determination began to rise.

I started to see that my real issue wasn't the loss but my resistance to accepting it. I was stuck because I kept trying to reverse what had already happened.

But once I accepted my new reality, the fog began to lift, and I was able to see blessings that had been in front of me all along. One of them: opportunity. It had always been there. I just couldn't see it because I was trying to solve a problem that no longer existed.

That realization became a conviction: even when the vision is unclear and the dream feels distant, some things are just common sense—make a decision, and take a step.

THE SHIFT

Growing up, I saw many injustices as I traveled across the country with my parents and siblings, who were migrant workers. I witnessed firsthand how the system favored some while making life harder for others—especially for people like me—no matter how hard we tried.

I also saw how that unfairness weighed heavily on a man's spirit, particularly those trying to lead and provide for their families. The pressure to remain strong in a system that constantly reminded them they weren't enough often led to silent suffering.

I saw it in my father and in other Black men around me. They wrestled quietly with questions of identity and worth, caught between what they were told they could be and what they knew themselves to be deep down. Denied opportunities, stripped of resources, and locked out of systems they couldn't access, they had few places to turn—and even fewer people to confide in.

For some, that weight turned inward, showing up as self-doubt or drinking to numb the pain. For others, it spilled outward—becoming anger, frustration, or even abuse. It wasn't always about wanting to hurt those they loved, but rather about having no safe outlet for the pressure that was breaking them from the inside out.

The real challenge wasn't the work itself; it was proving we belonged. We had to fight for every step forward, even after proving ourselves worthy of the spaces, roles, and conversations we were constantly excluded from.

Relying on that same system, asking for work and seeking approval, often felt like swallowing bitterness.

But what choice did I have?

The answer was clear: my family depended on me to act.

Even if the system wasn't built for me, I refused to let that stop me from doing what needed to be done for those counting on me.

Before going to sleep on the third night, I set aside my frustrations with "the system" and held on to one belief: that God had a plan, even if I didn't understand it yet. I woke up early on the fourth day, determined to find a job, telling myself, "I'll take the first offer that comes my way. At least I'll have a paycheck."

The first place I visited was Evans Construction, and they offered me a job.

The superintendent said, "I'll pay you $2.25 an hour if you can do what you say."

I knew I could handle the work and more, so that wasn't an issue. I started the next day.

After several weeks on the job, I noticed the houses were being built faster than they could find workers to clean them. That's when it hit me. They needed someone right away to clean the houses, collect the trash, and haul it away.

Since I still had the truck from my previous business, I was already equipped to take on the work. One day, I overheard the foreman and a few superintendents talking about the problem, trying to come up with a solution.

Without waiting for an invitation, I spoke up. "I'll do it."

Brian, the foreman, looked at me and asked, "How are you going to do that? You already work eight hours."

"I'll do it early in the morning before work, and late at night after hours," I replied.

He nodded slowly. "I'll ask Wade," he said. Wade Morris was the owner.

The next day, Brian pulled me aside and said, "Wade told me, 'As long as he gets his regular work done, he can do the job. I don't care when he does it.'"

Then Brian added, "He wants to know how much you'll charge."

THE COST OF OPPORTUNITY

When we discussed the job details, they made it clear they would only cover labor and reimburse dump fees. That wasn't typical, because most agreements also accounted for gas, vehicle wear and tear, and travel time to and from the dump.

I knew the terms favored them, but I didn't argue or complain. I stayed quiet and focused on the work. This was my chance to recover some of the income I'd lost after the company closed, and I wasn't about to let pride stand in the way.

This wasn't just a lesson about them—it was a lesson about me. I was learning to lean into difficult situations, especially when life didn't go the way I hoped. Even when the conditions weren't ideal, I began to see that the best choice was often to keep moving forward and make the most of what was in front of me.

I was beginning to understand that things don't always go my way—but they can still work in my favor.

I provided the estimate, and they accepted the offer. I started each morning at 4 a.m., cleaning two houses before my scheduled eight-hour shift. When necessary, I'd head home for dinner with my family, then go back out to finish the job.

I was working hard to rebuild stability, but I wasn't just logging hours—I was paying attention, eager to learn, and determined to grow.

HATE HAS NO SHAME

I was fascinated by every project around me and eager to learn, often watching subcontractors handle electrical work, install windows, and hang drywall. But what captured my attention most were the fireplaces; I couldn't stop watching the crews who built them.

While most of my co-workers spent their lunch breaks chatting and swapping stories, I'd grab my sandwich and wander the jobsite, soaking in every detail.

It was thrilling to see an architect's vision take shape, phase by phase. I didn't have a clear plan for my own life beyond the work I was doing, but I was naturally driven to understand and improve.

Still, my curiosity wasn't always welcomed. Some of the more experienced workers mocked me, calling me slow and stupid. But their words didn't discourage me; I kept showing up, eager to learn more.

The fireplaces, in particular, puzzled me. I couldn't figure out how a fireplace could be in one part of the house while the chimney was in another.

So I asked one of the older workers, "Mr. G., how does a chimney draw smoke?"

He chuckled and said, "Son, you're a young, hardworking man, but this is beyond you."

The others laughed, and for a moment, their laughter rang louder than my question. But in that instant, I thought to myself, *Nothing is beyond me. If one man can do it, I can too. I just haven't figured it out yet.*

That encounter changed me.

Even now, I avoid asking direct questions. Instead, I steer conversations to uncover what I need to know indirectly. And if I want to learn something, I'll find it in a book.

From that point on, I studied relentlessly. I picked up every book I could find and read it, no matter how long it took. I gathered whatever broken bricks I could get my hands on from the jobsite to practice building fireplaces in my backyard. I'd build one, tear it down, then rebuild it again and again, honing my skills until I understood every part by heart: the structure, the ratios, the function.

But I didn't stop at building. I also taught myself how to estimate the cost of constructing one.

And through it all, I learned something deeper: you don't always need to understand why something happens—or even ask. Sometimes, you just have to trust that the situations you're placed in are shaping you for what's coming next.

LIFTING THE BURDEN

I was making progress in my life, but I couldn't ignore the fallout from my client's bankruptcy. The impact on the cement company that had extended me credit weighed heavily on my conscience. Even though I had every reason to move on, I knew the right thing to do was to keep my word. My company was gone, but my integrity remained.

To my surprise, just three weeks of cleaning houses was enough to completely pay off the debt. That payment brought a deep sense of relief—an assurance that the worst had passed.

A few weeks later, I received a thank-you letter from the concrete supplier. He confirmed receipt of the payment and expressed his surprise and appreciation for my dedication to honoring the debt.

He wrote, "Only you would follow through on your commitment." He also promised to help me if I ever needed support.

That letter represented more than a settled account. It was about honoring relationships. I was learning how to apply God's word to real-life situations and discovering the blessings that come with respecting His instruction.

Romans 13:8 says, "Owe nothing to anyone—except for your obligation to love one another." Keeping my word and paying my debts wasn't just a moral duty: it was a spiritual law. If love is the only debt we're meant to carry, how are we demonstrating that through our commitments, especially when they come at a cost?

I reflected on Proverbs 22:1: "Choose a good reputation over great riches; being held in high esteem is better than silver or gold." I wanted my children to carry a name they could be proud of—one that would yield respect and make their path a little smoother.

At the time, I didn't fully grasp it, but integrity isn't just personal—it's generational. It's about laying a foundation for my children and shaping a future built on the values I hoped they would carry forward.

But that hard-won sense of stability didn't last. Soon, a disruption forced me to reconsider everything. Once again, it changed the course of my life.

HOLY DISRUPTION

For about three months, everything went smoothly—until the day I found myself working alongside the foreman's brother, David. It didn't take long to learn that he was earning more per hour than I was.

What he earned didn't trouble me. What concerned me was that his output was lower and his work inconsistent. Meanwhile, leadership consistently praised my speed and precision, commending me for never sacrificing quality. Yet despite all that recognition, I was still earning less.

The more I thought about it, the more I began to wonder if those compliments were less about appreciation and more about strategy—meant to keep me focused on praise while distracting me from the real issue: my pay.

Here's why that quarter mattered: twenty-five cents per hour might seem small, but over time it adds up. In a week, that's $10; in a month, $40; and in a year, $480. Over five years, it totals $2,400.

With every passing year, that financial gap grows as your physical strength and stamina decline. Keeping up becomes harder—while those small differences in pay build into massive disparities.

This kind of injustice—often hidden—continues to widen the wealth gap between races, genders, and other groups, benefiting some while pushing others further behind. What I had seen growing up, I was now living firsthand.

I knew asking for a raise would be delicate, so I approached the conversation with intention. Given the steady stream of positive feedback I had received, asking for a twenty-five-cent raise felt not only reasonable but long overdue.

I approached the foreman.

"Brian, I want to talk to you about my pay," I said. "Do you think I could get a raise?"

As if he had expected it, he smiled. "No problem. How about a nickel?"

"Not quite. I was thinking more like twenty-five cents," I replied, trying to stay firm but respectful.

Brian's smile faded. "No, that's as much as Dave is making," he said.

I didn't back down. "What's wrong with that? Don't I deserve the same?"

He hesitated, then replied bluntly, "Yeah, but you can't make as much as Dave."

My pulse quickened. "Is that because he's White and I'm Black?" I asked, my voice steady even as frustration rose.

"You said it, I didn't," Brian replied, a smug smile spreading across his face.

I felt a surge of anger, but I knew I couldn't let my emotions take control or react on impulse. I couldn't afford to risk my livelihood, or put my family in jeopardy again, by earning a reputation for being hot-headed. In small communities, word traveled fast, and we weren't planning to move out of state.

I took a deep breath.

"If that's the case, I won't work here anymore," I said firmly. "I refuse to work under circumstances where you have to be White to earn what you're worth."

As I walked to my truck, my heart pounded. Images of my family flashed through my mind, and the pain of losing my business still hung heavy. I didn't know how long it would take to find another job, so I slowed myself—mentally and emotionally—to figure out my next move.

My pride pulled me one way, but my responsibility as a provider pulled harder. I reminded myself that Brian wasn't the boss and didn't have the final word. So I made a decision: I would go to the office and speak with Mr. Morris.

As I walked away, I stayed focused on what mattered—what I needed for myself and my family. I didn't mention my conversation with Brian; I kept my attention on the goal: securing a raise that matched my output.

When I made my case, Mr. Morris responded without hesitation. "No problem. Just talk to Brian."

"I already talked to Brian," I said.

"What did he say?" he asked.

"I could get an additional five cents," I replied. "But I asked for twenty-five cents."

"Okay," he said. "I'll be out there in a few minutes, and we'll talk."

Relieved, I left the office and returned to the jobsite, thinking everything was going to work out. Mr. Morris wasn't far behind, but as soon as he arrived, Brian spoke up.

"He quit," Brian said flatly.

I didn't say a word. I didn't realize it at the time, but I was living out Exodus 14:14: "The Lord himself will fight for you. Just stay calm."

Mr. Morris responded immediately. "No, no. Bill can't quit—we have too much work to do."

"Don't worry about him. He'll be back in less than a week. He won't be able to find a job anywhere else," Brian said with a sarcastic grin.

His words struck a nerve so deep that my entire body tensed. It wasn't just the insult; it was the implication that without them, I was nothing, that my future was in his hands and there was nothing I could do about it.

As I listened, it was clear: they thought I was only worth the crumbs they chose to give me.

With steady resolve, I looked Brian in the eye and said, "Before I come back here to work, I'll pick up a rock and knock a rabbit in the head every morning to feed my family."

As I spoke my final words, everyone grew silent. Without another glance, I turned and walked away. It might have seemed like this was a decision about a job, but God was reclaiming something far deeper—my identity, my voice, and the blueprint He already held for my life.

PAUSE + REFLECT

God's plan doesn't always align with your timelines or desires. It's woven like a tapestry—each life serving a purpose far beyond what you can see.

When you focus too much on doing things your way, you risk missing the real blessing: aligning with His plan. God's perspective stretches beyond your personal hopes; it includes the stories, struggles, and prayers of every person on earth.

What may feel like a detour could actually be a divine adjustment, shaping your story to fit His greater purpose. And within that plan, there may be moments when you feel unseen, your effort overlooked, and your potential dismissed.

Yet these are the very places where courage begins to take root. When you act with conviction instead of chasing approval, you draw on the strength God has already placed within you.

REFLECTION PROMPTS

- When have you felt underestimated or dismissed by those who should have seen your worth? How did you respond?

- What truth about your identity have you silenced that God is calling you to reclaim?

  _____

  _____

  _____

- Where is God urging you to move forward with courage, even when the path feels uncertain?

  _____

  _____

  _____

RECLAIMING THE BLUEPRINT

HEALING THE WOUNDS, REBUILDING THE VISION

*That's why I take pleasure in my weaknesses, and in the insults,
hardships, persecutions, and troubles that I suffer for Christ.
For when I am weak, then I am strong.*

II CORINTHIANS 12:10

WHEN PAIN HAS A PURPOSE

I climbed into my truck and drove for hours, talking to myself without finding answers. How could I go back home, look Shirl in the eyes, and burden her with the fact that I didn't have a job—again?

I thought about everything she carried.

By twenty-six, in just nine years, she had given birth to our four children, supported me through four job changes (soon to be five), moved house three times, and managed every detail of each transition.

With every move, Shirl turned the house into a home. She cleaned, organized, and held our family together while I worked long hours chasing what I thought was our next step forward. She never asked how to handle my absence; she simply did. I knew it wasn't easy, even though she never let it show.

Shirl didn't just endure—she led with unwavering strength. She packed my lunch, kept dinner warm, and rose at any hour to serve me. More than the tasks, it was her spirit—grace in the grind and peace under pressure—that brought stability to the chaos and gave me space to keep pushing ahead.

Even knowing all she had done with and for me, I understood that leaving that job wasn't about twenty-five cents, or Brian, or Dave, or even an unfair system. It was about the arrows still lodged deep in my heart—some I pretended didn't hurt, others I tried to forget, but none had ever truly left.

I had taken arrow after arrow, burying them beneath hard work, perseverance, and the instinct to survive. I told myself I was fine, that I had moved on. The truth was, I hadn't healed. I had only learned to tuck the pain away and function through it.

And then I thought back to the little boy I once was, picking cotton in the field while a group of young White boys stood at the end of the row and shouted, "I wouldn't be a nigger for thousands, millions, or billions of dollars."

My mother looked at my siblings and me and said, "Hold your peace."

I did. But I carried it.

I carried my teacher's cutting words—"You are the stupidest boy I've ever seen."

I carried the whispers that told Shirl I'd never be more than a potato picker.

I carried Mr. G's dismissal of my curiosity as mere amusement: "This is beyond you."

That day in the truck, something clicked.

This pain—these arrows—weren't just mine alone. They were rooted in generations of fear, prejudice, and deeply ingrained beliefs. And more than that, God was allowing me to carry this weight not only for my own growth, but for His glory.

Here's the truth I could no longer ignore: without challenges, I didn't need a champion.

As I drove, something began to awaken inside me. I wasn't fragile—I was strong. And this wasn't about ego. It was about identity. My identity wasn't limited to my past or my circumstances—it was anchored in who I was becoming.

How far was I willing to go with God?

As Paul wrote in 2 Corinthians 12:10, "That's why I take pleasure in my weaknesses, and in the insults, hardships, persecutions, and troubles that I suffer for Christ. For when I am weak, then I am strong."

That day, I heard God speak clearly: "You built before. You'll build again."

The moment those words settled in my spirit, I knew my answer. I turned and headed home.

Looking back, I can see the pattern now. I met God in stillness and surrender: in a field when I gave my life to Christ, in my sleep when I learned to read a blueprint, and in the quiet of my truck when I was forced into silence.

God works with each of us in His own way. For me, it's always been in the quiet—not just for comfort, but for commission. That's when He gives the next instruction. It's in the stillness, that sacred space where surrender deepens, awareness sharpens, and vision expands. It is in those times that I hear Him most clearly and find the courage to act.

This time, what He was building in me wouldn't rise overnight. It would require endurance, wisdom, and the kind of trust forged in private long before it's seen in public.

BUILDING FROM THE BLUEPRINT

At thirty, with past pain behind me and a renewed sense of purpose pulling me forward, I told Shirl—pregnant with our last child—that I was going to rebuild the business.

She asked why, her curiosity gentle and sincere. I explained, and she responded as she always had: with full support and belief in me, even though success didn't come overnight.

For two weeks, I took on odd jobs, whatever I could find. It wasn't ideal, but I earned more than I had at my previous job. That time taught me something important: just because God is leading you doesn't mean results will come right away.

As Hebrews 11:1 reminds us, "Faith shows the reality of what we hope for;

it is the evidence of things we cannot see." I began to understand that faith isn't just what I believe—it's how we live.

There were no shortcuts. I had to keep going one step at a time, leaning on the promise of Jeremiah 1:5: "I knew you before I formed you in your mother's womb. Before you were born I set you apart." I didn't fully grasp what that meant, but Psalm 119:105 offered clarity: "Your word is a lamp to guide my feet and a light for my path."

Slowly, the vision started to take shape. Odd jobs turned into steady work, and soon I found a rhythm. I'd drive without a map, following a quiet nudge that led me into a neighborhood or down a street where someone needed concrete poured, a step built, or a sidewalk repaired.

It wasn't easy. The pressure was real. We welcomed our fifth child, a son, in the first year of rebuilding the business. There were plenty of prayers and uncertain moments. But in the middle of it all, my pastor shared a spiritual principle that transformed my thinking.

A SPIRITUAL CHALLENGE

One of the biggest shifts in my life came through my former pastor, Rev. Hart. While working on the church, he and I would sit and talk. He was a man of vision and heart who saw what was happening in my life and kept pointing me back to a simple truth: faith is revealed not just in what you earn—but in what you give.

One day, he challenged me directly: "You think you're doing something, but you're not doing anything." Then he added, "Have more faith in God. Put more into the church—your time, your money—and watch what He does."

Through those conversations, my pastor taught me how to live God's Word by understanding spiritual principles. One in particular became central to me— Luke 6:38: "Give, and you will receive. Your gift will return to you in full— pressed down, shaken together to make room for more, running over, and poured into your lap. The amount you give will determine the amount you get back."

I considered his words carefully, but what convinced me wasn't his message—it was how he lived. I watched him give away his paycheck and, just weeks later, return with a testimony. A stranger would show up with exactly what he had been praying for.

I wasn't giving to get; I understood that you can't outgive God. But that seed was planted. And when I began acting on it, everything started to shift— bigger contracts came, closed doors opened, and Shirl and I found ourselves living in abundance again.

Living the principle didn't bring instant success, but over time, the ripples became waves. The income followed the same pattern—it grew from nickels to dimes to dollars, then to hundreds, thousands, and eventually hundreds of thousands, as work started stacking up in ways I'd never imagined.

It took about four years for the business to find its rhythm. By then, I wasn't the little guy anymore. I was the one in charge. I didn't get everything right. I still don't. And I certainly didn't have it all figured out. But it was enough for God to start shifting people and power dynamics around me.

Remember Brian, the superintendent who refused me a twenty-five-cent raise? When he and Dave were both laid off, I hired them—and paid them double their previous salaries.

When I was hired to build my first fireplace, I completed it without issue— no safety concerns, no design flaws. In that moment, I realized that building fireplaces had never been beyond my abilities. And neither was hiring Mr. G and his son. It wasn't about proving a point—they were skilled builders, and I had a business to run.

Years later, the teacher who once called me "the stupidest boy I have ever seen" became my neighbor, building her home right next to mine. One afternoon, as we stood in my yard making small talk, she said, "I always knew you would do well."

I reminded her of what she'd said when she was my English teacher. She looked at me, smiled, and replied, "Oh, I would never say anything like that."

Psalm 110:1 says, "Sit in the place of honor at my right hand until I humble your enemies, making them a footstool under your feet." I held no hatred or resentment, but I'll never forget how God revealed Himself—just as He promised. And neither did they.

This journey was never just about personal success. That was only one visible outcome. What truly mattered was how I received and responded to what God was doing within me.

In many ways, our walk with God is an input-output journey. The output doesn't always come automatically; it depends on how we understand, receive, and respond to what He's telling us. His provision, presence, and promises are already with us, waiting for our faith, our surrender, our yes.

When we begin to move with Him, even imperfectly, something shifts. Quietly and steadily, what's happening on the inside begins to show on the outside. For me, that included rebuilding the business. But more importantly, it was about being rebuilt—slowly but deeply.

PAUSE + REFLECT

When the arrows of your past remain lodged in your heart, it's easy to anchor your identity in the wreckage. But sometimes, God calls you to reclaim your vision and rebuild from the very pain that once tried to define you.

Recognizing your wounds isn't weakness; it's a courageous step toward healing. When you surrender them to Him, He can transform that brokenness into the foundation for something greater. In His hands, pain becomes purpose, and you gain the strength to build again.

REFLECTION PROMPTS

- What painful voices or past labels still echo in your mind? What would it take to release them and move forward?

  _____

  _____

  _____

- Where is God asking you to rebuild—even in the face of fear, fatigue, or past failure?

  _____

  _____

  _____

- How has your pain prepared you for purpose? What brave act of faith can you take in response?

_____

_____

_____

CHAPTER 6

WHEN HEAVEN RELEASES

THE EARTHLY EVIDENCE OF A DIVINE PLAN

*Oh, how great are God's riches and wisdom
and knowledge! How impossible it is for us to
understand his decisions and his ways!*

ROMANS 11:33

S. RENEE'S MOMENTS TO MEASURE

CHAPTER 6

This is the moment you realize that everything that happened to you was actually happening for you. The disappointments that bruised you, the delays that frustrated you, and the detours that confused you were all preparing the way for something greater.

When Heaven Releases isn't just about success—it's about divine positioning: being exactly where you're meant to be when the doors open. It's about spiritual maturity: learning to see God's purpose in every situation. And it's about visible impact: the kind that transforms not only your life, but the lives of those around you.

In Lessons 16–18, you'll learn to:

- Recognize the moment when God says, "Now," and how your response shapes what comes next.

- Identify, respond to, and nurture the divine connections that unlock purpose.

- Understand how faith and action work together to turn divine opportunities into real-world outcomes.

- Give and serve in ways that position you as a vessel for legacy-building impact.

NOT A PLOT, GOD'S PLAN

KNOWING YOUR NEXT STEP

The Lord directs the steps of the godly.
He delights in every detail of their lives.
Though they stumble, they will never fall,
for the Lord holds them by the hand.

PSALM 37:23-24

Whether I was on the mountaintop or in the valley, God was always there. Every delay and breakthrough formed part of a rhythm only He could compose.

But I began to wonder: *Was I following His lead, setting my own tempo, or co-creating the melody with Him?* I believe I came into the world already wired for it. My job was simply to listen, tune in to His frequency, and let my steps fall in line.

Still, my actions revealed a deeper question: Was I walking with God, or was He walking with me?

When I started my business the first time, it felt like God was proving Himself to me. Like the early days of any relationship, trust was forming. Each encounter pulled me closer to what I wanted and what I knew I needed.

My heart was open. My faith was strong. I was fully receptive to what God would do.

But somewhere along the way, I stopped seeking His answers and started stepping to my own beat. I suffered the consequences of moving out of sync with Him.

Whether missteps or milestones, self-imposed or preordained, they were exactly what my soul needed to mature. Still, it's heartbreaking to know that when I leaned into my own understanding and trusted my opinion over God's, it impacted others, just as their decisions impacted me.

Even so, I believe God allowed just the right circumstances to wake me up, to remind me I wasn't listening anymore. During that time, I still went to church, prayed, praised, and served, but I was on autopilot. Like any relationship you begin to take for granted, you assume the other person will always be there, even when you stop listening and responding to them.

That's where I found myself—in that place where I had stepped away, out of alignment with God. From moving in and out of that cycle, I learned this: I didn't lose the business the first time; I got out of alignment.

I know this because three or four more companies went bankrupt or said they couldn't pay me, yet I was able to withstand those losses. Ecclesiastes 3:1 answers my questions about timing, trust, and transformation: "For everything there is a season, a time for every activity under heaven."

Just like that six- to eight-month period when I lost my vision but not my drive, growth is a cycle that repeats itself. It requires us to let go of the old, embrace the new, and graduate to a higher level of spiritual awakening. If you embrace the process, each time, you'll go deeper.

But here's what I missed, and what I hope you see clearly: the process isn't meant to make you lose faith, but to grow it. Rebuilding the business the second time took longer, not because God had stopped moving, but because I had started second-guessing myself. I carried a quiet caution, questioning not just the path but my ability to walk it.

We often talk about seasons as "good" or "bad" depending on how they feel. But I wonder how much our opinions are shaped by how we believe others see us. I've come to believe that all seasons are good, because each one holds purpose. Some are just harder to navigate.

Even then, God is aligning us with what's next. Sometimes it's exactly what we hoped for. Other times, it's what we never saw coming. Most often, it's something greater than we can imagine. During the four years I spent rebuilding, I could feel something stirring beneath the surface. But I can't point to a single day when everything changed.

Here's the lesson: It's not about plotting your next move in advance. It's about cultivating alignment—so when His timing arrives, you'll recognize it. And when that moment comes, the difference between missing it and moving with it often comes down to one thing: How you respond when Heaven speaks.

SPEAK WHEN YOU'RE SPOKEN TO

As my faith grew stronger, so did my confidence. By the fifth year, the business was thriving. Within seven years, I began to embrace a vision of new possibilities—not by pushing harder, but by intentionally listening again.

Then a call for proposals from one of the world's largest coatings companies grabbed my attention. I thought about my growing team—an executive assistant and nearly twenty-five men, each with a family to support.

I was carrying more than just my own hopes. When you run a business, your employees may clock out, but your pressure doesn't. You're always thinking about the people who depend on you. And when something big like this comes along, you ask yourself: *Can this help us go a little further?*

The next day, I drove up to the mostly empty lot that would eventually become the home of a two-story warehouse. At the time, there was only a trailer, wheels still attached, with a short set of steps leading to the door of a temporary office.

Inside, a staff member greeted me and accepted my $500 check in exchange for the blueprint and instruction booklet. The packet outlined the project's rules and timelines and explained how each contractor's work needed to be completed to ensure success.

After reviewing the blueprint and reading through the hundred-plus-page manual over several days, I carefully planned how we'd pour, level, and protect the concrete. There was no room for error. Delays came with a $1,000 penalty on the first day and an additional $200 to $250 each day after that.

I reviewed everything again to calculate and submit my final estimate. A few weeks later, I received a letter inviting me to the contract award meeting. I was both pleasantly surprised and a little disappointed. I just wanted to know: Did I get the contract or not?

When I arrived, I learned I was one of four finalists. I could tell they were surprised to see me. Understandably so: I was a stranger to this group. Companies that operate nationwide typically bid on projects of this size. My work was limited to the East Coast, from Pennsylvania through Maryland.

As I walked into the office, I realized: I had crossed a line many wouldn't even dare approach—and with good reason. Between the application fee and the enormous time commitment needed to review material and prepare a proposal, the process can be overwhelming.

I knew it was a long shot—and that this was a door only God could open. But I also believed it could be evidence that nothing is out of reach when you trust Him. As Jesus says in Mark 10:27: "Humanly speaking, it is impossible. But not with God. Everything is possible with God."

The four of us were led into a small room with no chairs. The company representative sat behind a long desk while we stood. No small talk, just business. As part of the elimination process, he gave feedback on our bids.

"You're too high," he said to the man on my right. The man nodded, said, "Thank you," and left.

"Yours is too low. It can't be done for that amount," he told the man to my left. He responded just as the first had.

That left me—and one other.

My heart leapt with anticipation. *Could I really land this contract?*

Then came the shift.

"Smitty, your estimate is the one we want to go with—but we're going to have to award it to Leo."

What? I thought, trying to make sense of what I'd just heard but not react.

Just moments ago, I was one of four. Now it was down to two, and somehow I was their top choice but not their selection. I wasn't upset, but I just needed to understand.

Before I could overthink it, I said, "You said I'm the one you want—but you're going to choose someone else?" I meant for it to come out as a question, but it came out as a statement.

"I don't think you have the support you need to do a job like this," he explained.

I pressed, "What do you mean?"

"Manpower, or the ability to finance the job."

"How much are we talking?"

"At least a million dollars," he responded.

I swallowed and took a deep breath. Calmly, I asked, "If I can line up suppliers to commit to that amount, would that change your decision?"

His face lit up. "Oh yeah—that would make a big difference."

I said, "Call Ray Cross, the owner of Cross Shift Contracting."

He looked surprised. "You know Ray?"

"Yes." I didn't say more.

He grabbed the phone and dialed Ray's office.

While he spoke with Ray, I was running through the names of other suppliers who might back me.

When he hung up, he looked stunned.

Turning to me, he said, "Ray said, 'If you're talking about Bill Smith, he can get ten million dollars of credit. Whatever he needs, I can supply.'" He smiled and said, "You got the job."

I was stunned. God had turned the tables before my eyes. This wasn't just about who I knew. It was about knowing when to speak, when to trust, and when to step forward. Luke 12:11–12 reminds us: "Don't worry about how to defend yourself or what to say, for the Holy Spirit will teach you at that time what needs to be said."

I can say this with confidence: God opens doors no one else can—and equips you with what you need to walk through them. But I'm a firm believer that faith alone won't get you there. Faith doesn't cancel your responsibility. It guides your action.

Genesis 3:19 says, "By the sweat of your brow will you have food to eat until you return to the ground." God is not your servant. If you want Him to move, you must be willing to move too.

If you wait for God to do everything while you do nothing, you'll be waiting a long time—just like I was when I sat at home for three days hoping something would change (Chapter 5, Lesson 13). God keeps His promises, but we must listen, learn, and act.

As Billy Preston sang: "Nothin' from nothin' leaves nothin'. You gotta have somethin' if you wanna be with me." That sums it up. God is looking for something to work with. James 2:17 says, "Just as the body is dead without breath, so also faith is dead without good works."

Even though I almost lost the deal due to perception, the superintendent later told me, "I've never worked with anyone who completed their portion of work ahead of time at every phase of the project."

None of this makes sense apart from 1 Corinthians 3:7: "It's not important who does the planting, or who does the watering. What's important is that God makes the seed grow."

Do all you can. Then let go and let God do what only He can. When you pray and praise, let those acts result in a shift in your mindset, beliefs, and behaviors. I'm not claiming to have a blueprint for success; I only share what I know from experience.

That one job didn't just bless us—it changed the trajectory of the business and our lives.

Not long after, another business owner called, requesting that we build four warehouses.

When I told him I'd need to schedule a time to meet and get the specs, but I was currently tied up and couldn't start his project right away, he said: "I'll wait. I don't care what it costs. I want you to do the work."

When the schedule cleared, I ran the numbers, sent over the invoice, and was paid on time. No questions. No delays.

God doesn't just open a door—He blazes the path forward.

PAUSE + REFLECT

God's plan rarely follows a straight path, and His timing often unfolds in surprising ways. You may recognize your season, but only God knows its full purpose. What looks like a harvest might actually be a time of pruning; what feels like a delay could be the exact pace He has set for your growth.

You may sense your next step, but the outcome isn't yours to predict. Still, it's essential to act when He leads because timing matters. Like fruit on a tree: pick it too early, and it won't taste the way it was meant to. Wait too long, and it will overripen, fall, and the moment will pass. In both cases, you miss what the season was meant to yield.

Recognizing your "now" isn't the end—it's the invitation. God may open the door, but it's your willingness to follow that carries you through. The words you speak, the courage you show, and the steps you take when His Spirit prompts you will shape how you walk out the opportunity He has prepared.

The goal isn't to map out every detail but to walk closely with Him so that, whether the season is pruning, planting, or harvesting, you hear His cue, trust His timing, and move when Heaven speaks.

REFLECTION PROMPTS

- Which word best describes your current season: pruning, planting, or harvesting? How do you know?

_____

_____

_____

- What recent situation could be God's way of calling you back into alignment with His truth and your values?

  _____

  _____

  _____

- How will you prepare yourself this week to move forward when Heaven speaks?

  _____

  _____

  _____

BEFORE YOU KNOW

WHEN RELATIONSHIPS
BECOME REVELATION

*Don't forget to show hospitality to strangers, for some who
have done this have entertained angels without realizing it.*

HEBREWS 13:2

GOD'S HAND IN HUMAN CONNECTION

We meet people every day—at work, in passing, in moments of crisis, and in what seems like a coincidence. Some stay for a moment. Others walk with us for miles—and a few become cornerstones in our story.

But how can we tell which is which—especially when our values seem misaligned or our paths feel too far apart? The truth is, we don't always know—but God does. Sometimes what seems ordinary is divine placement, and what appears to be just another person could be the start of a lifelong blessing.

Ray's unexpected endorsement—ten million dollars in material credit—wasn't just generous; it was jaw-dropping. But it wasn't a miracle that fell from the sky. I'm not a theologian, but both Scripture and my life have shown me this: God doesn't create spectacle. He acts with precision and purpose. What feels sudden to us is often something He's been faithfully arranging over time.

If we pay close attention—especially to the people and moments we often overlook—we might catch glimpses of what He's doing for us. That day in the trailer when Ray vouched for me wasn't just favor. It was a respected voice saying, "He's not just qualified—he's proven in character." That kind of trust is rare. It's built over years, through moments when your word, your work, and your walk all align.

Ray and I didn't talk daily or go on vacations together, but over time, something sacred was built—something only God could arrange. Ray saw more than a man with whom he did business or someone with a contract at stake; he saw a man with conviction. And what he gave wasn't just credit. It was confidence.

That's the kind of favor that can't be bought. When it's built under God's hand, it becomes more than a friendship. It's provision with a purpose.

A SOVEREIGN SETUP

I believe God's plan for Ray and me to meet was in motion before I was born, but I can trace it back to the day I walked into the cement and block plant in Wilmington around 1961. I was looking for a special type of block. I only needed three or four of them. Ray and his brother were talking, so I looked around until Ray turned and asked what I needed.

"Hey, young man, what are you looking for?"

"I'm not sure what it's called," I said, "but this is what it looks like."

"I don't know what that is," he replied, "but go in the yard and see if there's anything you can use. If you find something, bring it in, and I'll tell you how much it costs."

It was quick. Ordinary. Forgettable—or at least, it seemed that way.

Two years later, while I was laying block on a new project, a car slowed down, backed up, and the driver called out, "Hey, young man! Don't I know you?"

I walked over, and he said, "You're the one who came looking for that weird block."

I smiled. "That's me."

"Looks like you're doing block work, pouring cement, and laying sidewalk. Can't we do some business?"

When I mentioned getting a credit application, he shook his head. "You've got credit. I'll put your name in the system. When you're ready for block, concrete, brick, or cement, just call in your order. You don't need to fill out anything."

I had always ordered my concrete and other materials from HA Supplies and Tools. But their trucks only carried three yards of concrete. Although they always sent enough trucks, the process wasn't as efficient as Ray's business. His trucks delivered at least eight yards—much better suited to the size of my jobs.

From that day forward, except during the months I worked for Evans Construction, I bought all my cement, concrete, and blocks from Cross Shift Contracting, and everything else from HA Supplies and Tools.

LOYALTY WITHOUT LINES

From my first order, our relationship grew. Ray was smart, generous, and confident. One of the things I appreciated most about him was our conversations. They were honest; he understood the racial and political climate of the time, yet he treated people with respect and fiercely defended those he called friends.

I remember an event at a prominent, growing hotel chain where he owned the local property. This was before the Civil Rights Act of 1964 was passed. Most places were still segregated, but not in Ray's mind. He invited me to political gatherings and gave me tickets to academic scholarship fundraisers, where I was often the only Black person in the room.

The first time I ever faced trouble was at Ray's hotel during a political event. The room buzzed with handshakes, small talk, and the clink of silverware on plates. Most people greeted me politely, but I noticed a man seated across the room. He kept glancing my way, studying me as he steadily sipped drink after drink.

About halfway through the event, his expression grew more intimidating. Finally, he stood, walked to my table, and stopped in front of me.

"You're Black, aren't you?"

I met his gaze. "Last time I looked in the mirror, I was," I replied.

His jaw tightened, and his voice sharpened. "Boy, don't you get smart with me." He pulled back his suit jacket to reveal the pistol at his side. "I'll arrest you."

I began to rise from my chair, but before I could stand fully, Ray was suddenly beside me—as if he'd appeared out of nowhere. He looked me directly in the eyes. "Bill, what's going on?"

I tried to speak, but he didn't wait. Ray turned around, grabbed the sheriff by the collar, and ushered him toward the door. I don't know what was said, but I saw Ray's finger point, and the sheriff was gone.

Ray came back and stood beside me. He didn't whisper. He spoke calmly, but loud enough for everyone in the room to hear: "Bill, if any of these rednecks bother you again, you call me. I'll take care of them."

That was Ray: fair, protective, and unafraid to act. At a time when most people looked the other way, he stepped forward. He didn't calculate the cost or weigh the politics; he simply stood with the people he called friends.

I thanked him and smiled. "Ray, I appreciate it. But I can take care of myself."

Looking back, I see it wasn't just about protection. It was about trust— the kind you can't buy, fake, or rush. The kind God weaves into the fabric of a friendship, knowing one day, it will carry more weight than you could ever imagine.

AN INVITATION TO MORE

Ray wasn't just a businessman and friend; he was well-connected and a high-ranking leader in the Republican Party. Although our relationship had nothing to do with titles, influence, or politics, one day, during an ordinary conversation, he surprised me with an offer that made me pause. I had to ask myself two questions: Did I want it for the right reasons, and would I take it?

"Bill, would you consider running for office on the Republican ticket?"

Me? Politics? I thought. *I'd never put those two words in the same sentence.*

"I don't know anything about politics," I said.

"You don't have to," he replied. "You've got the respect of your community. I've checked your record. People believe in you. We could get every Black person to vote Republican."

I appreciated his honesty. No backdoor fluff.

I paused. It wasn't the idea of politics that made me hesitate; it was what I thought it implied. I knew Ray had good intentions. I also knew enough to recognize when I was being offered a position for my face, not my voice.

The next time I saw him, I followed up. "Ray, I gave it some thought. I don't think I want to deal with politics."

He nodded. "That's fine."

And that was it. He never brought it up again. Our friendship didn't change because what he wanted for me was different from what I wanted for myself, and we were both fine with that.

I believe Ray truly thought I would do a good job. But more importantly, he respected my decision. That moment deepened our bond. We could see, share, and live our own truths without losing respect for each other. And when I needed him, he was there. Always.

PAUSE + REFLECT

God's greatest provisions often come wrapped in people. Some will stand with you when it costs them something. Some will speak for you when your voice isn't in the room. Others will risk their name so your purpose can move forward.

Moments like these remind us that relationships aren't just social connections—they're divine assignments. And when they are, they come without manipulation, without keeping score, and without fear of loss.

Trust is the currency of God's kingdom. When it's built under His oversight, it becomes a channel for resources, opportunities, and protection that no amount of striving could earn.

REFLECTION PROMPTS

- Who in your life has stood with you at personal cost to themselves? How have you honored that trust?

- Are there relationships you've treated as casual connections that might actually be divine assignments?

- Since trust is the currency of God's kingdom, what are you doing to invest, grow, and safeguard your relationships?

_____

_____

_____

SAME HEART, DIFFERENT PATHS

WHEN SERVICE BECOMES SACRED

Work with enthusiasm, as though you were
working for the Lord rather than for people.

EPHESIANS 6:7

ABOVE THE NOISE

Some of the most sacred work Shirl and I have ever done didn't happen behind a pulpit or inside a sanctuary. It happened on jobsites, at a university, in unexpected encounters on the street, and in the kind of moments where service wasn't planned but lived.

As Proverbs 21:2 reminds us, "People may be right in their own eyes, but the Lord examines their heart." That scripture reminds me that our opinions, and even our actions, can't stand alone. It's the condition of our hearts that reveals our alignment with God.

This kind of love is louder than labels. It transcends race, religion, gender, or status, revealing a truth I've witnessed again and again: there is far more good in the world than all the noise would have us believe.

But seeing one another through God's lens takes compassion and understanding. That kind of spiritual purity and emotional generosity takes work. It requires humility and the willingness to learn from people—especially those who challenge us, stretch us, or see the world differently than we do.

God's assignments rarely come in perfect packages. More often, they come wrapped in flesh, not formulas. They show up in relationships and often reveal things about us we aren't ready to see. Shirl and I believe generosity is a core spiritual principle. Whether you're swinging a hammer, wiping a brow, listening to the heart of someone hurting, or writing a check, Proverbs 11:25 promises: "The generous will prosper; those who refresh others will themselves be refreshed."

We've found that when you serve from that place—without judgment, expectation, or self-interest—something shifts. Service becomes more than a task. It becomes worship.

LEVERAGING GOD'S KNOWLEDGE

By 1978, before I was forty, we had built and moved into a new home more than twice the size of our first. I don't share this to impress you but to testify to how God honors faithfulness. His provision didn't just expand our business; it expanded our capacity to serve, give, and grow.

As time went on, I built a reputation that opened unexpected doors. Doctors, judges, lawyers, and leaders across industries began calling on me to build their homes—not because I advertised, but because word of trust travels.

General contractors sub-contracted their masonry projects. Cities contacted us to provide concrete and brick work around monuments, and even government agencies and universities requested us to build structures.

And when I couldn't figure something out, I listened and leaned on God's knowledge, whether for stone, brick, or fireplaces.

I remember when we were hired to build a fireplace unlike anything we had done before. It had curved lines, sharp angles, and intricate design details that went far beyond our typical work projects.

I had a mason with over twenty years of experience leading the build, and my son was working as his laborer. But after two days of effort, they reached a dead end.

"This can't be done," Chris, the mason, said.

But I've learned not to get frustrated when someone says something can't be done. Instead of reacting, I quietly reminded myself, *There's no such thing as "can't be done."*

When I looked at the plans and saw the site myself, I understood why they were struggling. I didn't have the answer either. So I did what I always do when I reach my limit: I prayed. I asked God for insight and clarity. While I waited, I sent the team to another jobsite. I needed time and space—not just to think, but to listen. A few days later, I went back to the house and stood quietly in front of the wall where the fireplace would go. I didn't pick up a tool. I just stared. Then, it happened. *Ah! That's how it works.*

I drove straight to the supply store, bought the exact materials I needed, and built the internal framework myself. Once the infrastructure was ready, I called the crew back in.

My mason took one look at what I had built and shook his head. "Boss, I never thought it could be done." That moment reminded me: just because you've never done something doesn't mean it can't be done.

Sometimes the answer comes quickly. Other times, it requires waiting, listening, and trusting that God knows what we don't. We're wrong if we assume God's silence means He doesn't understand what we're going through. I've lived long enough to know: He sees. He knows. And He will speak.

It's simple: just say, "God, I need help," and wait for His response.

WHEN THE WORK IS WORSHIP

In the seventies, when our home church needed to move to a new property, options were limited. We couldn't afford to build or buy something new, so the only feasible choice was to split the existing building in half and relocate it about thirty miles.

Most "experts" warned us not to try it, and at first, I agreed. I didn't know how to move a building, and I wasn't sure it could even be done. The pastor and the members trusted me, so I listened closely, and when God provided clarity, I moved forward.

I asked Ray to donate blocks, concrete, and cement, and he did. Before that project was even finished, Pastor Hart approached us with another challenge: could we host a statewide event for the African Methodist Episcopal churches? We would need to build a building to feed the guests. As lead trustee, I encouraged us to say yes.

It took guts and grit. I was running my company during the day, and the other men had full-time jobs, too. But at night and on weekends, we showed up at the church with the vision on paper, dust in the air, and a few of us staying late while most went home. We worked side by side, and once again Ray provided materials. In just eighteen days, the hall was ready, and we hosted the conference. Fifty years later, both buildings still stand. It was no small feat. We didn't all do the same work, but we shared the same heart, and God used every part. That's how the work gets done.

As I think about Ray, the first blocks were his gift—the foundation we built and the friendship we shared for twenty-seven years. Ray passed in his mid-fifties, but his impact still stands. Some friendships don't end with death; they echo beyond it.

A few years later, under a different pastor, the congregation generously named the building the William J. Smith Sr. Community Hall. For that, I'm forever grateful. But that wasn't the end of the story. In fact, it was just the beginning.

POSTURE OVER PORTION

Over the years, Shirl and I have looked for ways to give beyond the church walls. Whether supporting hospitals, museums, or associations, we said yes whenever we sensed it was right.

What began in a field with faith and hard work became the foundation for how we live: building what lasts and giving to what matters. One example is the scholarship fund created in 2010, now an endowed fund housed at Shirl's alma mater, Delaware State University. It's our way of planting seeds in students we may never meet, because impact isn't always measured by what you see, but by what you sow.

But here's the thing: it's not about how much you give; it's about what's given from the heart. To me, it's a combination of spiritual purity and financial generosity.

During Shirl's time pastoring a church, one of the church mothers smiled after a small birthday gathering, wished me a happy birthday, and pressed a damp napkin into my hand. Inside were coins—thirty-eight cents. I paused, realizing she had given me everything she had. In that moment, the lesson settled deep: generosity isn't a number; it's a posture.

I still have the thirty-eight cents, wrapped in that same napkin. It also reminds me that we don't all give the same way. Some swing the hammer; others carry the prayers. What matters is that we offer what we have—and God weaves it all together.

HEAVEN'S ASSIGNMENT

While I can't say this with certainty, I believe very few people—outside of close family and friends—continue to live in your story, or you in theirs, long after they've passed. That's when it becomes clear: family isn't just defined by earthly circumstances but by divine appointments. And when Heaven speaks in those moments, you'd better be listening.

It was around 1961 or '62, and we were still living in the trailer. The owner of the gas company made a habit of driving around to check on his customers, not just to ensure they were satisfied but also to keep an eye on his drivers.

That's how we met. One morning, he pulled up in front of our trailer, and we struck up a conversation. With a slight stutter and little warmth, he asked, "What do you do?"

"I do masonry work," I replied.

He listened, nodded, and went on his way. A few weeks passed, and then the phone rang.

"You want to do some work?" he asked.

"Sure," I said.

"Can you meet me at my office tomorrow at 10 a.m.?"

I arrived early and waited. Eventually, he walked me through the office and pointed to a wall.

"I want you to cut out this section and install a window. Can you do it?"

"Yes, sir."

That same day, I cut the blocks and installed the window. Once I finished, I let him know.

He seemed surprised. He walked down the hall into the room and examined my work from every angle.

"Nice job," he said under his breath. "I'll pay you now."

I told him the amount due.

He looked at me and said, "That's a little high, ain't it?"

"I don't think so," I replied.

Without another word, he turned to his office manager and asked for a check.

About three months later, he called again—this time asking me to pour a concrete pad for one of his gas stations. We met at the site where he pointed his finger, mumbled a few instructions, and then drove off.

When the work was finished, he came to inspect it and with minimal comments gave his approval. And when I handed him my invoice, he looked at it and said, "That's a little high, ain't it?" I didn't respond. He returned with my check, and what he said next took me by surprise.

"I've got stations and properties all over," he said, pausing. "I need concrete and other work done. I want someone I can trust, someone I can call, and they'll take care of it."

Then he looked me in the eye. "Do you think you can do that?"

"Yes, sir. I can."

From that day forward, I handled all his work for the next twenty-six years, until he retired. He wasn't much for words. When he did speak, it was either a question with only one right answer—his—or a command that left no room for discussion.

His usual way of giving instructions was straightforward: meet you at the location, point his finger, mumble a few words, and drive off. For larger projects, I'd prepare drawings to make sure we were aligned. He'd glance at them briefly and say, "You know what you're doing."

From the moment the job began, he'd ask over and over, "Will you be done tomorrow?" He didn't care what the real timeline was; he just wanted to hear "yes," and most of the time, he'd walk off before I could even respond.

But in his own way, he demonstrated he trusted me. He never asked for an estimate and always paid whatever invoice I sent.

SEEING BEYOND THE SURFACE

People often asked, "How do you work for that 'mean old' man?" I'd just smile. He wasn't mean, just different. And being different didn't make him wrong. It made me better—more patient, more understanding, more capable of meeting people where they are.

I'd often ask myself, *How can I improve my working relationship with Mr. Kingsman?* Matthew 23:11 says, "The greatest among you will be your servant."

I wasn't coming from a place of ego or comparison; I simply wanted to serve. I believe we can get along much better than we think. The key is understanding that most of the time, people don't mean harm by what they say or do. And when they do, it's usually not worth responding to.

Assuming someone acted deliberately is giving them a level of self-awareness they probably don't have. More often than not, they haven't given you—or the situation—much thought at all.

Some communication experts—including my daughter—teach how to read people based on behavior. But my question is this: what if we stopped interpreting body language, stopped filtering words through our own pain, and simply accepted people as they are—with no expectation for them to be different?

If we did, maybe all the boxes we put people in would disappear. And what would that leave us with? Acceptance? Peace? Grace in action? Everything is relative, yet some truths are universal. But just as Judas betrayed Jesus with a kiss, we can just as easily be fooled by a smile as we can misjudge a frown.

That awareness has helped me connect with hundreds of clients over the years, each with their own nuances I had to learn and understand, and with thousands of people I've encountered along the way.

I learned this early. Some call it wisdom. Others call it a "superpower." Throughout my thirty-seven-year relationship with Mr. Kingsman, we had only one conflict, and it happened when I responded in frustration to a question he often asked: "Will it be done tomorrow?"

Instead of staying calm and recognizing the pattern, I snapped and said, "If you want it done by tomorrow, get someone else to do it."

He fired back, "You're fired!"

So I packed up my tools and went home.

The next day, he called and asked, "Why aren't you on the job?"

I simply said, "I'll be right there."

I'd been working for him for about sixteen years when his wife passed away. About a year later, he pulled up to the jobsite, and I saw a spark in him I hadn't seen in a long time. That's when he introduced me to his new wife. I remember the moment clearly—she was sitting in the passenger seat, reading the newspaper.

She was warm and gracious, asking about the people working for me. When I pointed to my three sons, she lit up, expressing genuine enthusiasm and joy. She admired seeing my family working together, and I think that meant something to her—maybe because her first husband had passed, and she didn't have children of her own.

Later, Mr. Kingsman told me she wanted me to do some work at their home. I did, and that marked the beginning of a deeper involvement—not just with him, but with her as well.

As Mr. Kingsman grew older, they both began to rely on me more—not only for work but also to help maintain their home and look after their well-being.

Over time, he developed a habit of sharing his life stories with me. One day, after I'd finished my work, we were talking as usual. Then Mrs. Kingsman came in and quietly sat down. The room shifted—just slightly, but noticeably.

That's when Mr. Kingsman said, "Bill, I need a favor from you." A stillness settled over the space. I wasn't sure what was coming next.

"Can I depend on you?" he asked.

"I'll do it if I can," I responded.

He looked at me and said, "I don't want to go to a nursing home. And I don't want my wife to go to one either." His voice softened. "Can you promise me that you'll take care of us until we pass?"

I paused and looked at him, then at Mrs. Kingsman, and said, "I promise."

Mrs. Kingsman turned to him and said, "Maybe you should put it in writing, and have him sign it?"

But Mr. Kingsman shook his head. "No. If Bill tells me he'll do it, he'll do it."

Eventually, when he could no longer care for himself, I'm not sure who made the arrangements, but one morning the doorbell rang. Two healthcare workers stood at the door.

Mrs. Kingsman directed them to give him a bath.

They weren't in the room five minutes when we heard him screaming and crying: "Bill! Bill! Bill! Get these people out of my house!"

Mrs. Kingsman looked at me.

"He's calling you," she said.

I went upstairs, and as soon as he saw me, he reached out and said, "Get these people out of my house. I don't want anyone taking care of me but you."

"Okay, Mr. Kingsman," I replied.

I turned to the healthcare professionals and simply said, "I got it." It was their first and last day. I called their supervisor to make sure she understood it wasn't about them—but we wouldn't be needing their services.

For about eight months, I cared for Mr. Kingsman. He stayed alert and talkative right up until about forty-eight hours before he passed peacefully in his sleep.

Afterward, the house felt quiet without him. I missed his presence and often found myself walking past old photos, recalling something he'd said or done—each memory deepening my appreciation for the man he was.

As I mourned his loss, I realized, much like with Ray, Mr. Kingsman and I had slowly built a foundation of mutual trust and quiet admiration. He would talk about how he got his start—how hard it had been in the beginning. He was delivering fuel with nothing but a five-gallon can. No truck. No team. Just him, doing whatever it took to build something from nothing.

During our conversations, he opened up about family dynamics and his hopes for himself and his loved ones. In those moments, I saw pieces of my father—and even parts of myself. Maybe that's why we connected. While others often found him abrasive, overly direct, or emotionally distant, I recognized something familiar.

It was the sound of someone waking up every day knowing the odds were stacked against them, but still showing up. Still fighting—for their family, their name, their dignity. And hoping for a sign that God was still with them.

As Romans 8:31 declares, "If God is for us, who can be against us?" You want your children—and grandchildren—to have something to start with. Even if it's just a name. One that makes people pause—not because of wealth, but because of the respect it carries. That's not about status; it's about integrity.

And contrary to what some may believe, that kind of respect isn't handed to you just because you're born White. When you come from nothing, no matter who you are, you have to earn it. The road is long—painful, lonely, sometimes heartbreaking, and often back-bending, but you hold on.

In his case, as a Christian, he believed that God hears, sees, and understands feelings that can't be put into words. When he spoke about what mattered most, I didn't just hear him—I saw him, felt him, and experienced it with him.

Ironically, at the core of my relationship with Ray, a Republican, and Mr. Kingsman, a Democrat, wasn't politics, but something far more personal. Despite their power and opposing views, both were willing to be vulnerable with me.

In the quiet moments—between decisions, behind closed doors—I witnessed their strength, but I also saw their humanity. They wanted the same thing: to make a difference, to leave something that mattered. What connected us wasn't our titles, but the quiet ache of the heart—the hope that when our time is done, our lives will have meant something to someone else.

Ten years apart, in the same month, two very different men became etched into my story.

And maybe God timed it that way to remind me: Heaven's assignments don't end when a person dies—sometimes, that's when they begin.

TWO MOTHERS, ONE SON

I continued working for Mrs. Kingsman, doing the same tasks I had handled before Mr. Kingsman's passing. Over time, she gave me more responsibilities, including greater access and more control over decisions that needed to be made around the house.

During quiet moments, she would sometimes say, "William, if I had a son, he'd be just like you."

It was kind to hear, but I didn't think much of it. I assumed it was simply her way of showing appreciation for what I was doing.

But one day, she surprised me. She looked at me and asked, "Would you mind if I adopted you?"

I paused.

Adopt me? I thought. *I'm a grown man. Can someone even do that at this age?*

Smiling in disbelief, I answered gently, "Mrs. Kingsman, that's not just my decision. That has more to do with my mother."

She met my hesitation with quiet seriousness. "If your mother says yes, will you agree with her?"

I thought about how my mother might feel. I knew it didn't change my love or loyalty to her—in fact, it felt like a way of honoring both women. But that was how I felt. The question was, how would she feel?

"Yes," I said. "If my mother says yes, I will."

Mrs. Kingsman called her that same day.

Later that afternoon, the doorbell rang, and I opened the door to find my mother standing outside.

"Mrs. Kingsman wants to talk to me," she said. "Is she here?"

"Yes, ma'am," I replied, walking her toward the living room. Mrs. Kingsman came out to meet her halfway. I stepped aside, closed the doors behind them, and went upstairs to catch up on paperwork.

About forty-five minutes later, I heard Mrs. Kingsman's voice call out, filled with emotion.

"William! She said yes!"

I looked at my mother, who turned to me and said, "I agreed under one condition: you never change your last name."

I nodded.

"You promise me you'll never change it," she insisted.

"I promise."

At sixty-four years old, I walked into the courtroom with two women who had shaped my life in distinct ways—one by giving me life and nurturing me from childhood, the other by building a deep bond of trust with me over many years. While she had always treated me as her son, that day, I legally became Mrs. Kingsman's son.

The judge looked at us and said, "Mrs. Kingsman, you now have all the rights and responsibilities of a mother, as if you had borne him. And

William, you now have all the rights and responsibilities of a son, as if she had borne you."

Then he said, "Mrs. Kingsman, take your son home."

She smiled, took my hand, and led me out of the courtroom.

I helped care for my mother during her sickness and had full responsibility for my adopted mother during her four years of illness. Interestingly, both of my mothers passed away on the same day, in the same month—exactly one year apart.

My birth mother passed during the night. One year later, Mrs. Kingsman passed on that same date, early in the morning, in the arms of my oldest daughter as she sang "Precious Lord, Take My Hand."

Looking back, having two mothers to love—and to be loved by—stands as the clearest evidence that heaven released something long before it ever reached me. It wasn't just a miracle; it was a divine calling. One that unfolded not through grand gestures, but through God's quiet invitation to show up, serve, and love without condition.

When heaven releases, it may arrive through signs and wonders—or through a whispered promise, an unexpected adoption, or the fragile cry of someone calling your name because you're the only one they trust.

That's when you realize you could never have imagined this life. And in that moment, you're not just grateful for what happened; you're humbled to have played a small part in God's holy plan.

PAUSE + REFLECT

Sometimes, what God is doing doesn't seem "Godlike" at all—especially when it comes through people you least expect.

The betrayals you didn't deserve. The people you trusted who left—or stayed too long. The paths that led to pain. If you only look for God in what you understand, you'll miss how He truly works. Because often, what looks least like Him is exactly where He's working most.

If you're honest, it's not God's power that trips you up; it's His process. The way He moves through mystery, through what feels like contradiction and even conflict, can be deeply unsettling.

But in time, you'll begin to see that those things, too, were part of a plan you couldn't yet grasp—until Heaven reveals it.

REFLECTION PROMPTS

- Could you give more freely? In what areas of your life are you holding back? Why?

- Have you ever overlooked someone or something because it didn't "look like God"? How might God be inviting you to see with new eyes?

- What relationship or situation in your life might require you to look beneath the surface before drawing conclusions? What do you sense God wants you to notice there?

_____

_____

_____

WHAT LOVE BUILT

THE POWER OF A LIFE
DESIGNED BY GOD

Now that I am old and gray, do not abandon me, O God.
Let me proclaim your power to this new generation,
your mighty miracles to all who come after me.

PSALM 71:18

S. RENEE'S MOMENTS TO MEASURE

CHAPTER 7

Some chapters of our lives don't end; they echo. Chapter 7 is about legacy, not just the kind carved in stone or written in a will, but the kind built through love, faith, quiet sacrifices, and long-held prayers.

It's the legacy that lives on through stories, choices, and the people we become.

Look What Love Built invites you to reflect on the life you've lived, the love you've received, and the spiritual inheritance you're being called to pass on. It may be the final chapter, but it's not the end—it's a sacred handoff between generations.

In Lessons 19–21, you'll learn that:

- Legacy isn't just what you leave behind; it's also what you pass on every day.

- Love shown, even if it's delayed, still holds the power to heal and transform.

- Failures don't erase your purpose; they reveal why it matters.

- Walking with God creates an impact that multiplies as we live for Him.

WHEN YOU'RE THE PROVISION

WHEN PRESENCE BECOMES PARTICIPATION

Dear children, let's not merely say that we love each other; let us show the truth by our actions.

1 JOHN 3:18

WHEN LOVE SHOWS UP

You have walked with me through the toughest lessons, the deepest questions, and some of the most sacred moments of my life. If there's one truth I want to leave you with, it's this: love—and how you express it—is what truly matters.

In these final lessons, I want to speak plainly, not about the events themselves, but about what they taught me. These are the truths behind the stories, the insights I hope you'll carry with you. They aren't just reflections; they're the essence of what I've come to understand—formed in quiet moments, shaped by family, challenged by life, and held together by God's grace.

These lessons weren't written at a desk. They were spoken from my heart—through tears, deep reflection, and love—on October 18, 2019, in Williamsburg, Virginia. It was a day I never imagined I'd witness, when God answered a hidden prayer: that my wife, sons, daughters, grandchildren, and in-laws would openly affirm that they truly love and care for me.

That moment began months earlier, when Shirl started planning an eightieth birthday celebration. She looked at venues, compared prices, and brainstormed ideas—until she paused and asked, "William, do you want an eightieth birthday party?" I told her I needed a few days to think about it.

As I reflected, my mind wandered through countless scenarios, but one question kept rising to the surface: *What if this is the only time I get to see all my children—and their children—in one place?*

That thought refused to leave me. Still, a big birthday bash didn't feel right. I didn't want the attention, the noise, or the crowd. What I wanted was simple: just my family.

So I told Shirl, "No. That doesn't interest me." Yet the longing lingered—a quiet, persistent desire to be surrounded by the people I love most, all in one room, while I still had the chance.

As my birthday drew near, S. Renee called and invited me to her and HL's home. I hesitated. Because a part of me still clung to the hope that my family might come to see me, and I couldn't bring myself to give my usual enthusiastic, "Yes!"

But the phone stayed silent. With each day that passed, hope dimmed. And eventually, I surrendered to a crushing fear: they didn't love me.

At the last minute, I decided to accept my daughter's invitation. I always feel the love in their home. When we arrived, HL mentioned that he and S. Renee planned to visit a military family the next day and asked if Shirl and I would join them.

The next day, when we reached the apartment building, S. Renee and Shirl went ahead and knocked on the door.

It opened.

S. Renee stepped inside, with Shirl close behind, and HL motioned for me to follow. I hesitated, a tightness forming in my chest.

"You go ahead," I said softly.

He turned to me with a grin. "Go ahead, Big Willie."

I whispered, "I don't know these people."

Still urging, he said again, "Go ahead."

I stepped through the doorway—and paused.

The room was still. All eyes were on me, and no one said a word. The faces looked familiar, but I couldn't quite place them. Maybe it was because I'd already let go of the hope that my family would come—making it harder to recognize what was right in front of me.

Then, just as the moment settled, I heard, "SURPRISE!"

It was like a gentle lifting of a fog. These weren't strangers; they were my family, my people, my legacy. In that moment, I realized love doesn't always arrive how or when we expect it, but it always shows up right on time.

I wept. When I thought I was ready to speak, I wept again.

Each time I thought I had gathered myself, the tears returned. Years of hidden, unspoken feelings pressed against my chest. When words finally came, they weren't polished—they were simply the overflow of a heart overwhelmed by love.

I wish the best for them—and for you. What I share here isn't a transcript of that day, but it carries the same weight, the same truth, and the same prayer: that love will silence your doubts, and that your life will speak louder than your words.

May the seeds planted in my family's hearts find a home in yours. I offer them now as both a testament to our sacred journey and a challenge—to go further with God.

That day, as I looked around the room, I saw living proof that legacy isn't just what we leave behind; it's who gathers when love calls.

ALL IN ONE ROOM

We gathered around the table at the resort house, some sitting, others standing. I was surrounded by those who had loved me at my best and felt my struggles most deeply at my worst.

Over the years, they had unknowingly caught my silent tears in their hugs, their smiles, and their words of admiration—just as I had quietly wiped away theirs by giving what I could, building a name they could stand on, and making sure they had a head start in the world.

They are my family: my wife, my children, my in-laws, my grandchildren, and—at that time—my only great-grandchild. These are the relationships God entrusted to me, and I gave them everything I had—whatever that looked like in the moment. My all was the best I knew, even when my choices didn't make sense to them—or to me.

But before there were many, there was one—and his arrival marked the beginning of everything I would come to cherish most.

It all began the day Shirl told me I was going to be a father. That moment became the proudest of my life. When I first saw my oldest son, I was just twenty-one years old, overcome with joy, awe, and a deep happiness. It felt as though I was looking at something greater than both of us—something Shirl and I had created together.

When I held him for the first time, the world seemed to fade away. No worries. No cares. Just me and him. I've never experienced anything like it since. In that perfect moment, I found myself asking, *What do I do now?* I searched for perfection within myself—not because I believed I had it, but because I wanted to give it.

Twenty-one years later, my grandson was born. Forty-one years after that, I held my great-grandson—four generations carrying my name. Three years and five months before his birth, during my eightieth surprise birthday weekend, I said I hoped to meet him. God answered.

"One generation commends your works to another; they tell of your mighty acts" (Psalm 145:4). Let me be clear: every child, grandchild, great-grandchild, and member of my family holds equal value. Continuity is a blessing, but no life is more important than another. The miracle is the love that unites us.

The true gift isn't merely living to see four generations; it's understanding that love is the thread connecting them all. Love breathes life into legacy.

BEYOND PAYCHECKS

If my words carry any weight, I hope they help you see what I didn't always recognize: your greatest gift isn't what you earn or the wealth you leave behind; it's who you become for the people you love.

For many years, I chased success, and I want you to succeed, too. You need to build a reputation and a life your family can admire and aspire to. But remember—true success isn't just about degrees, jobs, or awards. It's about staying united and growing together, nurturing love, trust, and connection while creating the stability and opportunities that help your family thrive.

While I got some things right, I didn't always know how—or have the space—to nurture deep, lasting love. And once you've gone too far down the road without it, building that depth becomes difficult.

For me, part of that stability meant providing. I've always made sure my family had what they needed to take a meaningful step toward the life they imagined. My wife would never have to worry about money or rely on anyone else—and that mattered deeply to me.

I think most parents share a common hope: that their children will start further ahead than they did. For me, that meant giving my family financial independence and a stronger foundation. I started with nothing—limited choices, scarce resources, and lessons I had to learn the hard way. I wanted something different for them: the freedom to pursue dreams by choice, not by necessity.

I share this because some of you may know this story from either side. Maybe you had a parent, spouse, or loved one whose way of showing love was to make sure you had more than they ever did—even if it meant being gone more than you would have liked.

This isn't an excuse; it's an insight. Sometimes, providing means being absent, not to abandon, but to create access to opportunities they never had. How that absence is understood varies. Some don't see it until they stand in the same place. Others may use it to explain their own pain or struggles.

We each get to choose how we interpret and judge our parents—or anyone who has shaped our path—and one day, our children will do the same to us. My hope is to break that cycle by offering understanding and insight, so that love—not misunderstanding—becomes the legacy we leave behind.

Provision isn't only financial. While paychecks matter, so do presence, guidance, and love that's tailored to each person's real needs. Show up intentionally—not just in the room, but through your family's daily rhythm. Teach discipline and the value of work, but also learn how each person receives love. True provision helps a family live well and navigate life with confidence, clarity, and connection.

As I reflect on what I could have given more of, I'm reminded of what I had to learn the hard way: how to love, and how to express it.

This kind of love demands vulnerability—the courage to face your silent disappointments, unspoken hopes, and deep desires for connection. It also calls for the bravery to share them honestly with those you love.

You may not hear, "I forgive you," the moment you say, "I'm sorry." And when trust has been broken, "I love you" might not be received right away—especially when both hearts are still healing.

Sometimes, we're ready to accept our part before the other person is willing to recognize theirs. Give them time. Give yourself grace.

Time alone doesn't heal wounds, but honest communication, consistent love, and the courage to grow can.

BREAKING THE CYCLE OF SILENCE

When you go out every day to fight—to prove yourself, to protect, to hold it all together—it becomes difficult to soften your heart. You stay ready for battle because you believe you have to be.

You tell yourself, *I'll rest later, talk later, feel later.* But later doesn't always come. Live that way long enough, and softening starts to feel dangerous, even at home, because you've lost the ability to access it within yourself. But open your heart, for their sake and your own, and something begins to shift. That day, with long pauses and tears, the tight ball inside me began to unravel. It was freeing.

They listened intently, hanging on every word, understanding the meaning behind each tear. And in their eyes, I saw relief—the recognition that I, too, was human.

Leaving home at a young age left me feeling alone in the world. That experience shaped me. It turned me into a survivor. It taught me how to work, how to win—but it also delayed my ability to love deeply, fully, and without fear. I'm still learning.

That's why I'm sharing this now. You have time to show up for the people who matter. Use it. Say the words you've been holding back. You may be afraid to tell the whole story or confess your mistakes—but you don't have to. I didn't.

I shared what I missed, what I learned, and how I want to move forward.

Even now, telling my story in this book has revealed steps I still haven't taken—not just in how I show up, but in how I express my love. It's not about dwelling on what I missed; it's about how I'll keep climbing—with greater awareness, deeper connection, and words that finally match the love I've always carried. I'm not focused on the past, but on the wisdom I've gained and how it shapes the way I love now.

My hope is that when you reach the fourth quarter of your life, you won't be haunted by regrets. Instead, you'll be surrounded by memories you created and the love you gave.

Of everything I've built and achieved, what fills me with the most pride is being surrounded by those I love. Sitting with my family that day, I felt like a balloon that had slipped from someone's hand, rising higher, feeling lighter, finally free to soar, no longer weighed down. I emptied my cup, and over the course of the three-day event, each of them filled it up again. I never thought I'd see the day when I could look around a room and know, without question, that everyone was there simply because they loved me. But when that moment came, all the insecurities I had carried for so long melted away.

I shared that I was reminded of how, as children, they expressed love so freely, before the world taught them to hold back. "Be a man. Toughen up." I learned that lesson, and in time, I passed it on to others.

Now, when I remember their young voices saying, "That's my daddy," I hear it differently. It wasn't just a statement—it was an offering of their hearts. I didn't realize how sacred that moment was. I heard the words, but I didn't always feel their meaning.

Too often, we don't fully appreciate love until it's gone. And I'm not just talking about the grief we feel when someone passes. I mean the love we leave behind each day—when we rush through life, avoid those we don't understand, or quietly hold on to resentment from unresolved conflicts.

Love slips away not just in loss, but in our absence—in silence, in assumptions, in our reluctance to speak. I know this now because I've come to see just how much love I've left behind over the years, not from a lack of caring, but from not knowing how to stay present with it.

The choices we make—whether born of fear, ambition, or simple misunderstanding—shape everything. They define how we grow, how we treat others, and what we're left to face when the end draws near.

That day, speaking openly didn't just break my silence; it shattered the pattern. I had finally learned how to express love out loud.

PAUSE + REFLECT

You might have convinced yourself it's too late to speak from the heart. Maybe you still believe that paying the bills and showing up when you could was enough. Or perhaps you've pulled away, assuming the people you love wouldn't respond with openness or kindness.

But here's the truth: it's never too late to redefine what love means. Never too late to be honest, to seek forgiveness, or to show up in a new way.

Saying "I'm sorry" doesn't always mean you were wrong. It can simply mean, "Having you in my life matters more than what happened between us."

Legacy isn't built on perfection. It's shaped by the courage to reach out, even when it's hard.

REFLECTION PROMPTS

- How has your past influenced your idea of provision? Where might it need to grow to include presence, love, or emotional honesty?

- What is one act of love you've been hesitating to do because of fear, pride, or past pain?

- Is there someone you've distanced yourself from who still needs more of you—or someone you quietly wish were more present for you?

REVELATION, NOT REGRET

LET LOVE BE LOUDER THAN YOUR FEAR

Such love has no fear, because perfect love expels all fear.

1 JOHN 4:18

WHAT I WISH I HAD KNOWN

This isn't an "if I could go back and do it again" message—it's simply a reflection on a few lessons I've learned from making wrong assumptions that led to poor choices. I don't have regrets, but I do have some revelations.

It all began with a realization: there's a clear difference between telling a story aloud and writing it down. Spoken aloud, my stories were entertaining; written on the page, they became enlightening—a mirror God used to search my heart.

Seeing them in writing made me pause and ask what was happening inside me—what fears, motives, and hidden struggles were at play. That honest self-examination started to change me.

We can't become who we're meant to be until we understand the internal forces that shape our decisions—and how those decisions, in turn, shape our lives.

When we examine ourselves honestly, we uncover our true feelings and begin to see the impact our actions have on others. Hurting the people who trust us can lead to numbness, hardness, or a quiet weight of shame, guilt, or embarrassment.

Even when we realize we've been wrong, we can be so committed to appearing right that we resist change. Instead of owning our responsibility, we dig in—justifying our choices, rationalizing the pain we've caused, or shifting blame. But freedom begins when we humble ourselves and take the hard steps to get back on track.

Deep down, we all want to see ourselves as good. But justification protects that image. The freedom we long for doesn't come from blaming others or clinging to past wounds—it comes from the courage to face the whole truth, trusting that grace will meet us there.

When your heart aches or your mind spins with regret, there's real freedom in honestly examining your life—because it's in that honesty that you begin to see God's hand at work, even in the mess.

Too often, we reach for spiritual clichés—"God's in control," "Everything happens for a reason"—because they feel easier than facing the pain. But pain, when unaddressed, quietly pulls the strings behind our choices, shaping our beliefs and behavior without us even noticing. We might avoid our real feelings, stay busy with religious activity, or agree with truth in theory while never letting it sink into our souls.

But here's the deeper reality: God is always sovereign, yet He never forces His way into places we won't open. The more we surrender, the more we experience His control working within us.

When we keep our distance from our true selves, we also keep our distance from the love and healing we crave most. Often, it's not just fear of others' judgment that holds us back—it's our own harsh self-criticism, or simply not knowing that a way forward exists.

As Scripture says in Hosea 4:6, "My people are being destroyed because they don't know me." Sometimes, we cling to pain or familiar patterns, unaware that knowledge, vision, and honest self-examination could unlock something new.

True healing comes when we can share our story with confidence—knowing we are free not only from guilt, but also from the pain that once led us into it. That's the gift Christ offers: not just forgiveness for what we've done, but wholeness for the places in us that have been hurting far too long.

This truth makes me wish I had eighty more years to apply what I've learned. And while I believe in God's power and know that anything is possible, I also know it's unlikely I'll be given another eighty years. What I can do, though, is leave these lessons with you—hoping you'll apply them now, while there's still time.

WHAT I WOULD TELL MY YOUNGER SELF

For a long time, I saw one of my hardest lessons through the lens of generational difference.

Just as my father had expectations for me, I had expectations for my children. I thought we were speaking the same language, just across different times. But over the years, I've come to understand that it wasn't just about age or era. It was also about access. What I mistook for generational change was, in many ways, a shift shaped by social and economic differences.

I started with nothing—no safety net, no fallback plan—just faith and determination. That reality shaped my hunger, my drive, and my view of what was possible. My children, by God's grace, began their lives on a more stable foundation. And when you grow up with options, the urgency feels different. The risks feel different. Even your view of what matters most can shift.

I didn't see that at first.

While my intentions were rooted in love, I was offering direction when what they needed most was space. I was trying to give them the outcome I had worked so hard to achieve—when what they needed was the freedom to define success for themselves.

That realization changed me. I had to let go of what I wanted for them, and give them what I had prayed for myself: peace, grace, and the freedom to walk with God at their own pace, in their own way.

I've learned a few things from being married, and I want to share them.

I didn't grow up hearing much about marriage. My father never sat me down to explain what it meant to be a husband—probably because he didn't know himself. That wasn't how most of us did things back then; we were just trying to survive, to make something out of nothing.

I remember him once telling me, "Find every dollar you can and stuff it in your pocket." For him—and for many in his generation—success was more than survival or security. It was about freedom, dignity, and the hope of building something better in a world where those things weren't guaranteed just because you were human. You had to fight for them.

Although much of our experience as a Black family was shaped by the unique challenges of our time, I've come to see that our struggles weren't ours alone. The fight for stability, respect, and opportunity has always crossed the lines of race, ethnicity, religion, and class.

It's not just a personal story; it's a human one. The lessons my father passed down reflected the realities of his era, but I believe people can change, and that understanding deepens as we grow.

What he taught me then was what he knew at the time, but we're all works in progress. Because of that foundation, my idea of being a husband was shaped more by observation and judgment than by real understanding. The things I saw and disliked, I swore I'd never do—without fully grasping why someone might have done them in the first place.

Still, I believed my father had at least part of it right: if I earned enough to pay the bills, kept the house warm in the winter and cool in the summer, put food on the table, and made sure my family had what they needed and wanted, then I would be a "good" husband.

But here's a warning: Judgment is a boomerang. As Matthew 7:1–2 tells us, "Do not judge others, and you will not be judged. For you will be treated as you treat others. The standard you use in judging is the standard by which you will be judged."

Looking back, I can see how deeply my life—and my marriage to Shirl—has been shaped by these early lessons. What we share is more than a partnership; it's a divine appointment. I am who I am because Shirl chose to walk with me, to love me, and to stay, even when I didn't always get it right. Her presence, her faith, and the promise I made to her stirred something in me, drawing me closer to God and changing the direction of my life.

Lately, I've come to realize I missed the mark—not out of neglect, but out of ignorance. When she tried to share her heart, I couldn't truly hear her. I didn't know the language, and my heart wasn't open enough to understand.

Even when she worked alongside me as my secretary, I assigned her tasks without ever revealing the full vision. She knew our income but not our debt. Though she supported me completely, she never saw the entire picture. At the time, I believed I was protecting her from unnecessary stress. But looking back, I can understand why she might have felt I was keeping her at a distance.

It took me far too long to realize this: inclusion isn't a burden—it's the gift of true partnership. When someone gives you their full support but only sees part of the truth, it can feel like being left out—even when that's not the intent. I see that now, and my heart aches for the pain it caused.

I probably never would have recognized it had *Go Further with God* not been written. I've asked myself over and over, "Who was this man? Who did he think he was?"

The truth is, I was stubborn. I did things my way, believing I was following God's lead. And because I kept succeeding, I assumed I was on the right path, doing the right thing, and never once questioned myself: not my thoughts, my decisions, or my actions.

But success can be a sign of God's favor, or a mask that hides misalignment. That's why you should never stop examining your motives or resist the wisdom of a healthy challenge. It's dangerous to never question yourself—or to discourage others from doing so.

Life and relationships aren't about insisting on your way. You bring your mind, your strength, and your gifts, but you also make room for, and honor, what your spouse brings.

Love isn't just about what you give; it's about what actually reaches the other person's heart. If they can't feel it, then to them, it doesn't exist.

True partnership requires shared responsibility: listening carefully, expressing your needs clearly, seeking to understand, and working together toward the best path forward. If you're not part of that process, you're not in a real partnership.

And in the end, you risk losing the very thing you wanted most and worked so hard to build: love. You can't go back and undo what's already happened, and neither can I. But we can choose to grow, to walk the journey together, and to go further as one.

These lessons aren't just for marriage. They apply to every kind of partnership—business, family, work, ministry—any space where two or more people are striving to create something meaningful. In every case, genuine partnership requires purpose, humility, and a willingness to walk in step.

My advice is this:

- Don't move so quickly that you lose the person walking beside you.

- Don't confuse provision with connection.

- Don't wait decades to say what needs to be said.

- Relationship success isn't automatic; it's intentional.

PAUSE + REFLECT

You might think, *I have time. I'll do it tomorrow.* But don't wait until it's too late. You don't need to say everything—just say something.

There comes a point in life when silence stops being a sign of strength and starts becoming a wall. We often wear our silence like armor, believing it protects us from pain, rejection, or vulnerability. But in truth, silence can create distance between us and the very people we long to be close to.

When love goes unspoken for too long, it starts to feel unreachable—either too far away or too much effort to reclaim. Breaking that cycle takes humility, courage, and the willingness to be vulnerable. It's not just about what we've done; it's about who we are.

You don't need perfect words—just a willing heart. Love speaks louder than fear when we choose to let it.

REFLECTION PROMPTS

- What are you holding back that your heart wants to say?

_____

_____

_____

- Where has silence caused distance in your relationships?

_____

_____

_____

- What small step can you take today to speak love more openly?

_____

_____

_____

You've heard my revelations; now hear from the one who walked them with me. Her words are the clearest window into how faith shaped our home.

ANCHORED BY FAITH, COVERED BY GRACE

REFLECTIONS FROM REVEREND SHIRLEY (SHIRL) M. SMITH

Father, I stretch my hands to Thee;
No other help I know.
If Thou withdraw Thyself from me,
O! whither shall I go?

These words have lived in my heart for decades. They speak to how we lived—how William led—and how God carried us through it all.

A LIFE LIVED TOGETHER

As William's wife, I was blessed to build with him, pray alongside him, and believe in him, experiencing God's presence in real time, up close, every single day. Again and again, I witnessed God's hand at work in his life.

William could barely read or write. He had no money and no connections. Yet from those humble beginnings, God lifted him to the top. He never focused on what he lacked; instead, he leaned into what he had: faith, a willing heart, and an open mind to what God could do.

SKILL, FAITH, AND DIVINE PURPOSE

I saw how God touched and transformed William's mind, turning what looked like limitations into a powerful ability to express God's greatness through human hands.

The homes, fireplaces, churches, commercial buildings, and monuments he built weren't just skilled craftsmanship; they were reflections of God's excellence. Some of those structures, nearly sixty years later, are still standing, still in use by third and fourth generations.

William wasn't just gifted with his hands; he was also gifted in how he listened to God. When he shared what God had shown him and I watched it come to pass, it was clearly divine, something no one could accomplish on their own.

He didn't just witness miracles; he understood their meaning. He didn't see one miracle and then wait around for the next to believe again. Instead, he embodied what God had already given him and worked faithfully to fulfill its purpose in his life, pouring everything he had into what he had been given, using it to the fullest before asking for more.

ANCHORED IN FAITH

With each blessing, my faith deepened, not just in what God could do, but in how He was working through William. I always sensed there was something special about him, and witnessing the magnitude of God's grace, mercy, and power in his life confirmed it. He is anchored.

By "anchored," I mean he believed in what he couldn't see and made decisions rooted in faith, not shaped by circumstances. His choices didn't always make sense to others, but they made sense to him—and that's what mattered. Once he sensed an answer from God, he stood on it, unshaken, because he trusted Him.

HOW DID IT HAPPEN?

All I know is this: our lives were rooted in prayer, God's Word, and trusting Him to lead us. What we learned in church didn't stay there: we lived it. We prayed at home, studied the Bible together, and watched as God answered prayer after prayer.

There was a natural rhythm between us, as if it had always been meant to be, each of us helping the other along the way. I never tried to place William where he didn't belong, nor did I hold him back from going where he felt led. That was between him and God. I simply made room for him to grow at his own pace.

After walking with William for over sixty-five years, here's what I've come to know: when you give God your life—your hands, your heart, your hopes—He'll take what feels small and turn it into something no one sees coming, not even you.

You've heard from my life partner. Now, as we wrap up, I want to speak to you one last time. This final lesson isn't just about reflecting on the past. It's about what you choose to do next.

A LEGACY
PASSED DOWN

LET YOUR LIFE BE THE LESSON

*And you must commit yourselves wholeheartedly to these commands
that I am giving you today. Repeat them again and again to your
children. Talk about them when you are at home and when you are
on the road, when you are going to bed and when you are getting up.*

DEUTERONOMY 6:6–7

Legacy isn't about holding on—it's about letting go, giving freely, and passing it forward. No story truly lives until someone else receives it and chooses to share it. Whether you're a family member, a friend, or a fellow traveler on this journey, make the lessons of *Go Further with God* your own. Share them. Live them. Let them grow.

As we age, life offers us more pauses—quiet mornings, waiting rooms, and the stillness that follows a new diagnosis. As our careers slow down and our children build lives of their own, we sometimes feel a quiet ache for the value we once carried. We struggle with no longer feeling needed.

With more time on our hands and less road ahead, we begin to look back. We measure our lives not only by what we've accomplished, but also by what we've missed, what remains unfinished, and the deeper meaning behind it all.

I don't know how much time I have left—maybe a year, maybe ten. God may grant me even more. But it's not about the time we have; it's what we do with it. As Abraham Lincoln said, "In the end, it's not the years in your life that count. It's the life in your years." That's the challenge I carry—and the invitation I offer to you.

Now, as we bring *Go Further with God* to a close, I can honestly say this journey has taken me places I never expected, surprising me at every turn.

It has revealed the immense depth of God's love—a love I still don't have the words to fully express. Not just His love for me, but for you, and for everyone. My heart has been opened to new ways of living and seeing, teaching me things about God I hadn't even considered. It's deepened my love for Him and my appreciation for my wife and our sixty-five-year marriage.

Along the way, I've developed a deeper reverence for these words from John 1:1–5: "In the beginning was the Word, and the Word was with God, and the Word was God. He was with God in the beginning. Through him all things were made; without him nothing was made that has been made. In him was life, and that life was the light of all mankind. The light shines in the darkness, and the darkness has not overcome it."

This Scripture is a reminder that my story, and yours, began in Him. Every step we've taken has been held together by the Word. The same light that carried me also lights the way for you. Nothing, not even the darkest season, can overpower it. It comforts me to know how deeply God loves us, and that through that love we can love one another.

And with that promise in mind, I pray this journey has both surprised and blessed you. I hope you realize now, more than ever, how deeply you are loved; that's the greatest gift you can receive, and the greatest gift you can give. You don't need many words to pass it on—just be love.

Real love leaves evidence. It shows up in how you protect, provide, forgive, and stay—especially when it's easier to walk away.

Here's my prayer for you: Gather as much love as you can. Carry it with you everywhere, and share it generously with others. Remember: once a moment, day, week, month, or year has passed, you can't go back and reclaim it.

Live love. Be love. And when the time comes, someone will look at your life and say, "Look what love built."

If these words help you speak sooner, love more deeply, or walk more closely with God, then every mile I've traveled was worth it.

When you wake up tomorrow, know that I'm grateful to have been welcomed into your life. And most importantly, remember that God loves you, sees you, and knows exactly where you are—meeting you in your story and walking with you as you write the next chapter.

Our stories are meant to be shared. The journey doesn't end with these pages. In many ways, it's a new beginning for all of us—as long as we don't close the book, or our minds, to what we've experienced.

If our *Go Further with God* message resonates with you, pass it on. Let your life be living proof of God's love—wherever you go and with whomever you meet. Sometimes, all it takes is a simple conversation or a gentle invitation for someone to realize they, too, can go further with God. That's how legacy grows. That's how we go further—together.

Whether our paths have crossed, will cross, or never cross, when my journey is finished and my body rests—if you think of me or come to say goodbye—know this:

> I am at peace.
> I am with our Lord.
> Thank you.
> I love you.

Go further with God—and take someone with you.

ACKNOWLEDGMENTS

FROM WILLIAM

- **To my wife, Shirley M. Smith:** To the wonderful woman who held our family together before there was anything to hold. The mother of our five children. My partner in poverty, prayer, and progress. You stood beside me when all I had was a dream. You never pulled back; you pressed forward with faith—carrying more than your share so I could carry mine. This book bears my voice, but it echoes the life we built together. Every page is evidence that God is with us.

- **To my children, William J. Smith, Jr., Wanda Kamethia Smith, Joseph L. Smith, S. Renee Smith, and Mark E. Smith:** You have been a blessing to me. There were seasons when I didn't know where I was going as I grew into myself. I made many decisions with each of you in mind, and each of you brought me something different. I know what each of you gave me—love, in your own way. I love you all very much.

- **To my grandchildren, Van Jermaine Smith, Tristan Renae, William Jefferson Smith, III, Virginia Marie Robinson, Jakeem Smith, and Julian Smith:** Each of you is my answered prayer and proof that love becomes a legacy. Stay close to one another. Speak love out loud. Forgive quickly and keep your hearts open. Build with courage, lead with kindness, and go further with God. May your lives be proof that faith works, love stays, and grace carries you home.

- **To my great-grandchildren and future generations, Tamia Smith, Zariyah Smith, and William Jefferson Smith, IV:** I'm thankful that God granted me the privilege of meeting you. Though the world is fast and noisy, some truths never change: the importance of integrity, the value of relationships, and the strength that comes from walking with God. Remember, you don't have to be perfect—just willing: willing to listen, to love, and to believe your life has purpose. Above all, know this: God has always been faithful to me, and He'll be faithful to you. Just trust Him. I love you.

- **To my sisters and brother, Elizabell Massey, Matthew L. Smith, and Alice Coleman:** We've laughed and learned from one another. I've had a wonderful life because you were part of it. Although we've taken different paths, I've carried each of you in my heart. Thank you for the bond we share. I love you all very much.

- **To *Go Further with God* readers:** Thank you for your time and trust. Sharing these stories healed parts of me I didn't realize were still tender—a reminder that God heals, provides, and redirects, often in quiet moments when we're finally ready to listen.

FROM S. RENEE

- **To my husband, HL Larry:** You are a force of nature, a presence that steadies me, strengthens me, and makes space for all of who I am and what I'm called to do. Your devotion to me; to my father, "Big Willie;" and my mother, "Momma Shirley"—names you lovingly gave them—isn't just spoken. It's felt. In your listening. In our conversations. In the meals you prepare. There were so many late nights. You'd call out, and I'd answer, "I'm coming, in a minute…" and still, you greeted me with love when morning came. This book carries my voice. But you created the space for me to speak and the strength to finish. —I love you

- **To my mom, Shirley M. Smith:** Writing Daddy's stories revealed yours—trust that held, love that stayed, belief that carried us. You gained a larger faith and laid down comfort and certainty to keep our family steady. You've loved us more than yourself, fighting for our needs, our peace, and our salvation so we'd make heaven our home. Thank you for your prayers, your kindness, and your steadfast heart. I am who I am because you chose love, again and again. I am your daughter, grateful beyond words.

- **To longtime friends and new readers:** Thank you for welcoming me into your home and my words into your heart. Walking through Daddy's story revealed how God meets us in the ordinary, grows us through pressure, and calls us to the next step. Take what you've gained here: clarity, courage, and deeper love. Apply it where it matters most, and ask yourself: *What's next?*

- **To the nine beta readers:** Thank you for volunteering your time and your best thinking. Your thoughtful reflections—spoken and unspoken—helped us go deeper and confirmed the heart of this message. Your written notes showed where the words landed and affirmed that we were on the right path. Thank you for walking this journey with us.

IN MEMORY OF

- **To my father, Benjamin F. Smith, Sr.:** It has taken more than fifty years since your passing for me to truly see you—and to understand what your life has meant to mine. You fought for dignity, demanded respect, and pressed against the limits others tried to place on you. You didn't just crack the door—you pushed it open and made space for me to walk through. I'm proud to be your son.

- **To my mother, Viola M. Smith:** Thank you for your unwavering love, gentle kindness, and for seeing me—especially when I couldn't see myself. As I reflect on my childhood, I see how deeply you cared, how fiercely you tried to protect me, and how much you gave in silence. I know now that the love and healing I received were not carried by your strength alone, but made possible by God's power and presence in your life. To God be the glory.

- **To the mother who adopted me, Eleanor C. Paradee:** You chose to call me your son—and for that, I am forever grateful. I love you for who you were—kind and understanding. I didn't always see it then, but now I understand: your gentleness was strength, and your kindness was how you shared love with the world. In your absence, your heart, humility, and values speak louder than ever.

- **My brothers and sister: Benjamin F. Smith, Jr., John Smith, James A. Smith, Roberta M. Potts, and Thomas E. Smith:** Though your earthly journeys have ended, your presence continues to live within me. I miss you deeply—and I love you always.

ABOUT THE AUTHORS

S. Renee Smith is a nationally recognized leadership strategist, personal brand architect, and executive coach who helps high-performing professionals live in what's next. She has built companies from the ground up to national recognition and has held leadership roles at Amazon and Walmart. Her contributions have been honored with S. Renee Smith Day by the City of Buffalo, a commendation from the Delaware House of Representatives as a personal-growth expert, and the Distinguished Alumni Award from the National Association for Equal Opportunity in Higher Education. Her work has also been endorsed by thought leaders including Les Brown, Jack Canfield, and Lisa Nichols.

She holds a certificate from the Wharton Executive Development Program and certifications through Gallup and the Society for Human Resource Management (SHRM). She is the author of five books, a coauthor of the *For Dummies* series—the world's bestselling reference brand—and the author of a communication book published by Sourcebooks.

As founder of the Leaders Career Accelerator, she integrates spirituality as the driving force behind authentic success. In *Go Further with God*, she brings emotional clarity, strategic wisdom, and spiritual depth to her father's remarkable legacy.

S. Renee speaks internationally, inspiring audiences to lead with purpose, grow in faith, and live in what's next.

William J. Smith Sr., founder and former CEO of Smith Masonry, Inc., led the company for more than forty years. A teenage runaway turned entrepreneur, he built his business from the ground up, leaving a lasting mark on residential neighborhoods, commercial developments, and sacred spaces throughout Delaware, Maryland, and Pennsylvania.

A lifelong member of the African Methodist Episcopal Church, William was also a devoted volunteer and faithful supporter of congregations in his community. A community hall he helped construct now bears his name, and an endowed scholarship at Delaware State University honors the legacy he shares with his wife, the Rev. Shirley M. Smith.

His story is a testament to God's quiet call, the strength forged through hardship, and the enduring power of perseverance guided by faith.

ALSO BY S. RENEE SMITH

There Is More Inside

The Bridge to Your Brand

Self-Esteem for Dummies

*Our Hearts Wonder: Prayers to Heal Your
Heart and Calm Your Soul*

Harness the POWER of Personal Branding and Executive Presence

*5 Steps to Assertiveness: How to Communicate
with Confidence and Get What You Want*

Thank you for reading *Go Further with God*.
We'd love to stay in touch.

Get bonus content, behind-the-scenes updates,
and spiritual encouragement at
GoFurtherWithGod.com

CONNECT WITH S. RENEE SMITH:
Website: srenee.com
Instagram: instagram.com/sreneesmith
Facebook Group: facebook.com/groups/gofurtherwithgod
LinkedIn: linkedin.com/in/srenee

SHARE YOUR JOURNEY WITH THESE HASHTAGS:
#GoFurtherWithGod
#SReneeSmith

www.ingramcontent.com/pod-product-compliance
Lightning Source LLC
Chambersburg PA
CBHW021140090426
42740CB00008B/869